**TALKING ABOUT MONEY IS LIBERATING.
THERE IS NO RIGHT OR WRONG WAY TO
HAVE THESE CONVERSATIONS; YOU JUST
NEED TO START.**

brazen

September 2021
Second edition

* * * * * * * * * * * * * * * * * *

Dedicated to you!
May you find your financial independence.

* * * * * * * * * * * * * * * * * *

First published in Great Britain in 2019 by Cassell,
a division of Octopus Publishing Group Ltd,
Carmelite House, 50 Victoria Embankment, London EC4Y 0DZ
www.octopusbooks.co.uk

An Hachette UK Company
www.hachette.co.uk

This revised edition published by Brazen in 2021

Design & layout copyright © Octopus Publishing Group Ltd 2019, 2021

Text copyright © Emilie Bellet 2019, 2021

ISBN 978-1-91424-023-2

A CIP catalogue record for this book is available from the British Library.

Printed and bound in the UK.

1 3 5 7 9 10 8 6 4 2

Disclaimer

MIX
Paper from
responsible sources
FSC® C104740

Contents

INTRODUCTION

A few years ago, I booked a meeting with a financial adviser. It would be the first real money conversation I had ever had. I was half excited, half wary, but I knew it was a necessary step on the road to adulthood.

I jumped on the Tube during my lunch break and navigated my way to the building. After a short wait and a quick glance at the *Financial Times*, I was invited to join the meeting by an assistant.

Good afternoon. Welcome, Mrs Bellet.

Thank you, good afternoon. Nice to meet you.

I tried to look relaxed but for some reason I didn't feel at ease at all. Perhaps this is always the case when you come face to face with a financial adviser for the first time, or perhaps I just felt like I didn't belong. Although I, too, was wearing a suit...

The adviser started speaking: *You're here to talk about financial advice. Do you know how it works?*

Looking at my blank face, he continued: *Oh, and where is your husband?*

This question sent me into a fit of rage. Did this adviser not think that I was capable of managing my own finances? Why on earth did I and my at-the-time partner have to do this together? Was I not good enough to work with this adviser? Was I not good enough, full stop?

Money is a feminist issue

On average, women who are in their 20s will retire with £100,000 less in their pension pot than a man the same age.[1] The annual pension income between women from an ethnic minority and white men is as high as 51.4%.[2]

The pension gap hurts women's financial futures, putting our retirement at risk. One of the reasons women have smaller pensions is the gender pay gap and the ever-increasing cost of childcare. High-earning, leadership roles are often incompatible with family life, which means that women take more career breaks and, inevitably, save less. We also make up the majority of people struggling with debt.[3]

Women tend to take fewer risks with their money, preferring to save rather than invest, which impacts retirement and long-term savings. Women hold £14.3 billion in investments compared to the £29.3 billion held by men, according to Kantar TNS.[4] However, women make great investors – a study by Warwick Business School found that women tend to outperform men at investing by 1.8%.[5]

It will take time to change the systemic inequalities, so it's important we focus on what we can do for ourselves in the meantime. When we are financially ill-informed, we are more likely to make poor choices that lead to negative consequences in our lives.

We are responsible for managing our finances

I started my working life in private equity for Lehman Brothers – an investment activity where a fund (a pool of money) buys and manages companies that are not publicly traded. On 15 September 2008, my employer filed for bankruptcy, which marked the start of a global financial crisis.

This made me aware of the huge financial literacy gap, the massive disconnect between banks and financial institutions and the public, the lack of trust and, at the same time, the huge responsibility for households to manage their own finances.

As a result, I set up Vestpod five years ago to help financially empower women. We organise events and workshops, host a podcast – *The Wallet* – and get women together to talk about money, savings, investing and debt.

Let's get the money conversation started

When researchers at University College London conducted a survey into sexual attitudes and lifestyle,[6] they found out that people were more inclined to answer questions about their intimate lives than questions about their household income.[7] And this is because talking about money is a deeply personal matter, which is often entangled with our emotional behaviour and feelings of self-worth.

But talking about money is liberating. Once you can talk about your finances freely, you can start to enter into non-emotional conversations about your own worth. Breaking the money taboo starts on the micro-level by talking with friends, family, strangers or finance professionals. There is no right or wrong way to have these conversations; you just need to start.

Slowly your financial awareness will start to kick in, and this greater understanding allows you to have easier macro-level conversations with your employer or others: to negotiate your salary, increase your freelancing rates, understand how your pension works and negotiate with your bank for a better type of card or with your lender for a mortgage.

Talking about money in relationships – whether that is with your partner, friends or colleagues – is the equivalent of facing the final frontier. Perhaps your partner has a massive student debt, you feel you're not being fairly remunerated at work or you and your friends find it difficult to talk about your budget woes. Whatever the issue, you need to brace yourself for these necessary conversations.

Your financial worth is not your self-worth

You're not here to pursue or accumulate wealth but to make sure you have enough to have the life you want. You want to make sure you're intentional with your money and don't feel pressured to spend when you don't want to or can't afford to.

Stop reaching for negativity when something goes wrong, be kind to yourself and start to believe that getting things wrong is a necessary stepping stone towards getting things (and keeping them) right. Altering your mindset from a fixed to a growth mindset will help you to become more rational about money and less controlled by your emotions.

Stop comparing yourself to others and recognise signs of FOMO (Fear Of Missing Out): no matter how successful you become, there will always be someone who has a bigger house, more extravagant holidays and greater financial security than you, so there's no need for external validation and to fit in financially.

Finally, focus on taking small, formative steps towards making your big dream achievable. Money can unlock many possibilities for you, and supporting the initiatives that you believe in makes you an activist with your money.

You need to uncover your money story

Have you ever wondered why you handle money the way you do today? Our spending and saving patterns are determined by our (sometimes limiting) habits, emotions and values, and what can really help us to reflect on our motives is to identify our money personality. We all have our own personal money scripts, which have been steadily forming since early childhood, and our money mindset has a direct effect on how we manage and deal with our finances.

Knowing your personality type can help you understand where you're starting from:[8]

- Do you feel that money can solve your problems or make you happy? (you worship money)
- Do you feel the pressure to 'fit in' with your peers? (you like status)
- Do you feel like money is an important topic to you, and are you working hard towards being financially secure? (you're money vigilant)
- Do you think negatively about money or think rich people are greedy and don't check your bank account? (you tend to avoid money)

Our beliefs have a knock-on effect on our ability to attain financial goals and financial security. But no attitude or behaviour is set in stone. Having a healthy approach to spending is something that you can build through greater financial education.

It's important to recognise that money helps us be independent; it's a tool, a form of exchange, that aids us in avoiding oppression while having control over our lives.

You're pre-rich!

You're Not Broke: You're Pre-Rich is not a book about getting rich quickly – it's about embarking on a journey, building healthier habits and supporting one another. It's about deciding on what you want, creating a plan and achieving it. While this book won't replace a financial adviser, it will help establish your financial literacy, which in turn will boost your confidence and empower you to achieve your lifelong goals.

Enjoy the journey!
Emilie xx

CHAPTER 1
GET REAL WITH YOUR MONEY

* *

What you will learn in this chapter:
How to do a financial check-up
If you have debt, how to deal with it
Who can help you in this journey

* *

In this chapter we will take a look at the big picture and start to get really intimate with your money! Don't worry, this needn't be overwhelming – because once you can see the reality and understand the factors that create these figures, there need be no more frightening debts, bills or standing orders lurking in the fringes of your bank balances waiting to wreak havoc on your finances.

Don't forget, the following does not constitute financial advice – it's just a set of useful tools to help you to understand where you stand with your money. You can always arrange to meet a financial adviser to get help on any of these topics (see page 24).

Financial Health Check-up

This section outlines how to achieve the transition from being broke to being pre-rich – which starts with understanding where you stand today.

Are you financially fit?

The difference between being broke and being rich is not related to how much you earn but to how much you keep – and therefore how much wealth you can build. We will call this your *net worth*.

Essentially, your net worth is a snapshot of your financial state of affairs and therefore your economic position. It normally refers to what you own (known as assets) minus what you owe (known as liabilities): *Net worth = Assets – Liabilities*. It will tell you how much money you would have left if you were to sell all your assets and repay all your debts 'today'.

Your net worth will vary over time, because your assets and liabilities will fluctuate. Monitoring your net worth is extremely empowering because it encourages you to take full control of your bank balance, financial health and ultimately your life. Understanding the numbers on your bank account statement helps you to become more rational with money, keep track of cash flow, set goals and focus on how your personal wealth is evolving.

YOU'RE NOT BROKE: YOU'RE PRE-RICH

What are assets?

Your assets are items of value that you own:

- *cash on hand*
- *real estate: house, flat*
- *bank account balance: current account*
- *savings*
- *shares, investments and insurance*
- *pensions and retirement savings*
- *the value of your business or start-up*
- *other assets: car, jewellery, furniture, anything of value that you own*

The value of your assets has to be accounted for at the current 'market value' (that means: how much you would get if you had to sell that asset today at current price) rather than the bought value (the price you paid for the asset).

What are liabilities?

Your liabilities are your debts, or the money that you owe:

- *mortgages*
- *credit card debts*
- *overdrafts*
- *student debt*
- *other personal loans: store cards, payday loans*
- *car loans*
- *other liabilities*

Don't panic if your net worth is negative and don't focus too much or judge yourself based on the result. Remember that your net worth does not define your self-worth. There are plenty of financially healthy reasons for having a minus total: perhaps you have a student loan or have only just started working. Understanding your current situation is a good place to start, so you can see what can be improved.

This exercise seems simple but when you actually do it, you'll realise that the hardest part is actually finding all these numbers: look at your bank and debt balances, find your pension log-in details. Maybe you'll add a placeholder in your calendar next Saturday morning, buy a nice workbook you can keep and get started with a good coffee! Make it a new weekly or monthly money date.

How often should you look at your net worth?

I think it is useful to calculate your net worth monthly or quarterly. Your objective is to see it increase in value from one period to another, so you know which direction it is going in. Remember this is for YOU only – you don't need to show it to anyone.

Building up your wealth

In theory, increasing your net worth is simple: you use your income (the money you make, for example from your job or investments) to increase valuable assets while reducing (paying off) your liabilities. Once your assets are worth more than your liabilities, you have positive net worth.

If you want to accumulate wealth, you have to focus on acquiring assets that will appreciate (increase in value) over time rather than creating further debt. Your goal is to have fewer liabilities (such as credit card debt) that cost you money (such as interest) and not to invest in items that will depreciate (lose value).

Your salary is only one way to build net worth (you might have another source of income from side projects or investments, for example). The big difference when you start trying to build wealth is that you start to generate money from other sources: your 'assets'. The goal, over time, is that these should generate more and more money and allow you to work less and less (and retire one day). True wealth is achieved by acquiring assets that will increase in value and generate money for you.

Of course, your liabilities will also increase because you are paying interest on them. Any outgoings that you are repaying over time, such as credit card debt, loans or a mortgage, will impact your ability to save and build assets.

Where to start?

We will look into the different ways you can grow your net worth in future chapters. For now, here are a few ways you can get started:

- **Build an emergency savings net:** If something unexpected happens, such as your boiler breaking down, you can dip into your emergency fund rather than take on debt (such as credit card debt) to pay for it.
- **Pay off some of your debts:** Focus on repaying the expensive debts first, i.e. those that are generating the highest interest rates, such as credit cards.
- **Top up your pension:** If you are not already contributing to your employer's pension or a personal pension plan, you could start now.
- **Reduce your spending:** Calculating your net worth can help identify where you spend too much money and enable you to cut out bad habits.
- **Grow your savings:** Keep an eye on your savings and potentially start investing for the long term.
- **Talk to a professional:** Speak to a financial adviser about your needs.

Be patient. Building net worth is a long process and does not happen overnight. There will be ups and downs and unexpected things can happen in your personal life (losing a job, moving to a new house, paying more rent, getting divorced) but this commitment to grow your net worth should remain. Use an online dashboard app to view all of your financial accounts in one place. Check whether your existing bank is also offering this type of service.

Are you creditworthy?

There is another 'number' widely used in personal finance: your **credit score**. While the net worth is your own personal number to measure your wealth, the credit score corresponds to your financial footprint and it measures how responsible you are with your money.

Your credit score is based on your credit history and how good you have been at repaying your debts. So credit can actually be a good thing, provided you handle it with care, because it eases your cash flow and allows you to have access to money to pay for things you need before the money is available. The way you use credit also gives financial institutions an indication of your financial health.

Why your credit score matters

Your credit score informs lenders of how robust and reliable you are. They then use this intelligence to try to predict your behaviour in the future, to safeguard themselves against your potential risk. Your credit score plays a key role in determining how much they will lend you and how much interest to charge.

For example, if you are thinking about applying for a mortgage to buy a house and you have a strong credit score and report, lenders will see you as reliable and the chances of you getting a loan are much higher. Added to which, if they see you as a reliable potential customer, they may also offer you a better mortgage rate too (that will cost you less money), helping reduce your monthly payments.

High credit score = Likely lower rate of interest charged on your loan, with the opportunity to borrow a higher amount of money.

Low credit score = Likely higher rate of interest charged on your loan, with the opportunity to borrow less money, and the danger that a bank will not lend to you at all.

The more visible you are, the more detail lenders can gauge about your financial stability and personality type. This can be infuriating if you are young or have never been in debt or never used a credit card because having no or little credit history can negatively impact your score.

How to get your credit score

Finding out your exact credit score is simple and quick. You can use an online credit agency such as Experian, Equifax (Clearscore) or TransUnion (Credit Karma) to do this. Try to use a free service and don't waste your money on a full report as the basic service is very good. Different credit agencies may sometimes provide you with a slightly different score so it is useful and good practice to compare your score with the other providers.

You can always ask to have a copy of your credit report for free – this is your legal right, as they hold lots of information on you.

Let's examine your report:

- **Your personal information:** Name, address, date of birth, whether you have registered on the electoral roll (this too can impact your score).
- **Your credit score:** This is your financial footprint.
- **Your debts:** Short-term as well as long-term: overdrafts, credit cards, payday loans, car loans, mortgages, personal loans and so on. The report will also include the payments you've made in full, late or actually missed. Note that student loans are not on your report and don't directly affect your credit rating, but some lenders can ask on their applications.
- **The search history:** Each time you ask for credit (that is, you want to borrow money or open a new bank account), the lenders will check your credit score. Lenders can see, from this section of the report, who has checked what, where and when.
- **Your financial connections:** Are you married and do you have a mortgage? Make sure you are associated only with people with a good credit history, otherwise their history could also impact yours. Check your address through an online credit agency to verify that your information is up to date. However, if you shared a bank account or mortgage with them, their credit rating may impact yours.
- **A report by Cifas:** This is the UK's Fraud Prevention Service and will highlight whether you have been a victim of fraud.

How to improve your credit score

Credit history is built over a long period of time, and while there is no quick-fix trick for improving your credit rating, you can definitely make a start.

- **Pay your bills on time:** Paying off your credit card balance in full every month is key but, if you really can't, at least make sure that you repay the minimum balance. Making late payments can negatively impact your score.
- **Maintain a low credit utilization ratio:** This is the difference between how much credit you are allowed and how much you are using. If you start maxing out all your credit cards, you will have a high utilization ratio – and will also be seen as someone who appears unable to manage debt carefully, and so may be unreliable. For you to look good, you need to aim for a low(er) utilization ratio, usually around 30%.
- **Reduce your outstanding debt:** If you have lot of outstanding debt it can be difficult for banks to lend you more money as they will be concerned about your capacity to repay.

- **Don't make repeated applications for new loans and credit cards:** Check your eligibility before applying.
- **Make sure you are registered on the electoral roll:** This is a simple and reliable way for lenders to verify that you are who you say you are and to protect against fraud.
- **Check your statements:** Make sure you check each entry on your account for any errors or inconsistencies, fraud or anything else.
- **Use your credit card in a good way:** It may sound counter-intuitive, but keep using that credit card – but make sure that you make payments regularly and do not exceed the 30% rule. The steadier your payment history, the easier it is for credit agencies to process your application. However, if you're not comfortable handling credit or using a credit card, stick to a debit card and avoid overspending.
- **Stop making cash withdrawals with your credit card:** Doing so can be recorded on your credit file; second, most providers will charge you a cash advance fee as well as daily interest (until you pay off the balance). Could you use a debit card instead?

There is a misconception that checking your score often is negatively impacting it; this isn't true, so keep on top of things!

BEWARE OF 'BUY NOW, PAY LATER' (BNPL) SCHEMES

Used correctly, these schemes essentially give shoppers the option to defer payments for items that they urgently need, while allowing the flexibility of paying in instalments. The appeal of instant gratification but delayed financial responsibility is indisputable and quite worrying, and people tend to spend more per purchase with these.

In the past, the lack of clear wording about the risk involved meant that many people ended up in debt. Under the new regulated plans, BNPL providers need to undertake affordability checks before lending to shoppers. Make sure you are making your own informed decision on whether or not BNPL schemes are for you.

Don't Let Debt Scare You

According to a report by the National Audit Office (NAO) and MoneyHelper, more than eight million people in the UK are said to have problem debt, i.e. they are over-indebted and can't repay their debts or bills. The other concerning statistic is that 22% of adults have less than £100 in savings, making them at risk if anything unexpected, such as an emergency or unemployment, happens.[9]

Debt: the good, the bad and the ugly

The first thing to know is that if you have debt, you are not on your own. Most of us carry debt of some kind. The second thing to remember is that having debt is not necessarily a bad thing.

The term debt is used very broadly but essentially it means owing money to someone. There is good, bad and ugly debt, and we all need to be able to understand the difference:

- **Good debt:** Is money you borrow for things that increase in value over time (student loans, mortgages, business loans). It usually bears a low(er) interest rate.
- **Bad debt:** Is money you borrow for things that lose value with time and is usually unplanned (impulse shopping on a credit card, payday loans, unpaid bills, money borrowed to pay for things you should have paid from your income or salary and are in a difficult position to repay). This debt usually bears a high(er) interest rate.
- **Ugly debt:** Is not an official term, but it is real enough. It relates to over-indebtedness, or problem debt, which develops when someone becomes unable to pay their debts or other household bills and debt become unmanageable (debt spiral, debt management, being unable to keep up with payments).

How debt works

To simplify your goal, when managing or incurring debt, you should focus on reducing bad debts and monitoring your good debt.

There are two main types of loan:

- **When your debt is secured:** It means that you borrowed money against something, such as your house. If things go wrong and you can't pay back the debt, the bank still needs the money back, so they may want to take the house (this is obviously a worst-case scenario). It gives the lender some guarantee.
- **When your debt is unsecured:** It means that you have borrowed money to spend on something that the lender can't take back: such as clothes, a holiday or something the bank is not interested in. These kinds of debts are often short-term and on a credit card.

Borrowing money can be helpful to progress and get the things you want in life: to educate yourself, buy property or pay for important things when you need them. If you are aware of how much you have, how much interest you pay on your debt and when you have to repay it by, then you are in the clear.

However, when borrowing gets out of hand, you can end up bearing a seemingly impossible burden. The level of interest can mount up fast and become very expensive, and gradually you find you can no longer pay the ever-increasing charges. At this point your debt becomes detrimental to your well-being and can lead to mental health issues, such as losing sleep, problems in relationships, absenteeism and lost productivity at work.

Credit card debt

When you use your credit card you are effectively borrowing money, which you can use to buy something you cannot afford or to ease cash flow. The crucial thing to understand is that the company that lends you the money does so because it makes good business sense to do so – you will pay them interest on it if you don't pay off your balance in full at the end of each month.

A credit card agreement allows you choose how much to repay – which can be extremely dangerous. A minimum repayment has to be made each month in order to avoid a late payment charge: this is usually set at between

1% and 3% of your outstanding balance. This is quite low and does not encourage you to repay your debt in full.

Credit card debt becomes bad debt only if it is not repaid in full at the end of each month. If you don't repay your credit card balance monthly, you will keep being charged an increasing level of interest, which is added to the total balance – it will be very expensive and you could lose control of your repayments. The less you repay one month, the less you are able to repay the following month, and things can snowball very quickly. Making low repayments will also have a big impact on your credit score.

The key to using a credit card is to use it only as a means to build your credit score and to ensure that you set up a direct debit so you don't miss the deadline for payment. You can usually set it up to pay the minimum amount, the outstanding balance (recommended!) or a fixed amount each month.

Credit card companies make their money from the interest you pay on debt, so they will increase your credit allowance, give you cashback and add rewards. Even though your income has not increased and your debt has not decreased, the amount you can borrow on your credit card has mysteriously gone up.

Two other examples of types of credit that are similar to credit cards are store cards and charge cards.

SAY A BIG NO TO PAYDAY LOANS

A payday loan is a short-term loan. The idea is that you can apply to be lent money quickly, for an emergency, and are then supposed to repay the debt on payday (even if this ranges from a few weeks to a few months). It is a very expensive way of borrowing because of the high interest rates, especially if you don't repay the debt within the fixed term of the agreement.

The cost of payday loans has now been capped by law, under rules made by the Financial Conduct Authority (FCA). The hope is that this type of loan will be banned completely.

Overdrafts

If you apply to the bank to borrow money that is not in your account, the bank is lending you money and you are falling into what is called an overdraft. Some bank accounts come with an authorized overdraft limit, but not all, so when you choose to open an account (see Chapter 5), make sure you check the overdraft limit and the interest charged.

TALK TO YOUR BANK

If you have problems with your credit card debt and/or overdraft, get in touch with your bank. They may suggest altering your overdraft limit, waive some of the fees on your account or help you to find a financial product that works better for you.

Mortgages

A mortgage is a debt that is arranged via a lender (usually a bank or building society) to buy a property. This debt is secured because, if for any reason something goes wrong, the bank can take back your home to repay the money you owe.

If you find that you are struggling to pay your monthly mortgage costs and you begin to miss payments, the amount of interest that you owe to the bank will increase – a lot. This can be the beginning of a difficult situation, as the bank could potentially take you to court and even repossess your house. However, those who have got into difficulty are often amazed at how helpful their lender can be. In order to prevent the worst from happening, make sure you speak to your bank or building society as soon as problems start. Build a plan to catch up with the payments and if you need help doing this, get further debt advice (see page 22).

Student loans

Student loans are less of a loan and act more like tax, because you only repay them if you have enough money (income) to do so. Of course, the repayments will impact on your available income and can make saving for other financial goals harder, but it has enabled you to pay for your studies and you should see it as an investment in your future.

Student debt grows with interest over time and, as soon as you start earning enough money, a percentage of your income will be deducted via your employer's payroll and paid to the Student Loans Company. This will continue until your loan has been paid off.

If you are self-employed, the amount you have to pay will be calculated in your self-assessment tax return (I recommend that you work on this with an accountant) alongside your taxes and National Insurance (NI) contributions. HMRC will then liaise with the Student Loan Company to inform them of your repayment.

You can also decide to pay more towards your student debt to repay it faster, but keep in mind that you could be using your surplus to go into other pockets, such as saving for your pension fund, or a home deposit or any other financial goal you may have. If you stop earning, the repayments will stop until you start work again.

Student loans get written off after a period of time depending on which repayment plan you're on. For more specific information about repaying your student loans, always check the latest information on the gov.uk website.[10]

Take back control

Managing debt is difficult and it can become a massive psychological burden, especially as it feels as though you are completely on your own. There is still a lot of shame associated with battling debt and it remains a bit of a taboo topic to bring up. As a society we are very limited in the way we talk about money and the emotional toll that worries and debt can take on professional self-esteem and mental health. But it needn't be this way. The best way to tackle debt is by taking small, incremental steps: dealing with one bill at a time.

By approaching repayments methodically, clear-sightedly (that is, not being in denial) and with a doable repayment plan, you should gradually repay your debt. It might take a while, but you will feel so much better, and more in control, knowing that every day you are getting closer to your goal. Plus, it will have the added bonus of giving a real boost to your credit profile.

Don't hesitate to ask for help – there are some great places where you can get FREE debt advice as well as phone support and online tools, such as Citizens Advice, StepChange Debt Charity, National Debtline and Mental Health & Money Advice.

Which debts to pay first

The first rule of getting out of debt is to make sure you are dealing with the most important debt first. Some repayments are more important than others because of the consequences of missing them.

Priority debts: Priority debts such as your rent, mortgage payments, council tax or hire-purchase fees should be paid in full every month. If you fear that you may miss a payment, contact your provider in advance to let them know and make an arrangement with them. If you can't pay them because you have too much debt, you need to get debt advice as soon as possible.

Non-priority debts: If you can't pay your non-priority debts, such as credit card debts, payday loans or overdrafts, your creditor could eventually take you to court or ask you for more money. It is important to keep the lender informed and to make an arrangement to pay at least the minimum amount on all debts to avoid falling behind.

1. **Stop blaming yourself – but do start taking responsibility:** This has nothing to do with your self-worth. It's maybe worth saying, 'I carry debt' instead of 'I am in debt'. Be practical and take action.
2. **Commit to not taking on any additional debt:** Before you do anything else, cut your spending. Stop using that credit card and remove your payment details from all retailers' websites! Freeze your card or cut it up. You have nothing to lose but stress.
3. **Face it and write it down:** Take a pen and paper and write down everything you owe. Make a list of all your debt on one sheet. Collate your latest statements, take a deep breath and open bills.

Find out the following:

- What non-priority debts do you have?

- What annual percentage rate (APR) are you paying on the interest?

- How much do you owe in total?

- What is your monthly payment?

- Order your debts, listing the debt with the higher interest rate first.

   You will now clearly know what you owe, in which area of your life your debts are located, the terms of the loan and interest payment due on each.

4. **Use a debt repayment method:** The most user-friendly debt repayments methods are:
- *The avalanche method:* When you allocate money to cover the minimum payment on each debt, and use any funds left over to repay the debt bearing the highest interest rate/APR; that is, the card that is most expensive is the one you pay off first. This method makes the most economic sense.
- *The snowball method:* When you allocate all of your extra money towards covering the minimum payment on each debt, and the extra money available then goes towards paying off the debt with the lowest balance first. If you feel overwhelmed at the thought of tackling all your debts at the same time, this method allows you to focus on just one.
- *The consolidation method:* If you're still struggling with the previous methods, you could look into consolidating all your debt into one payment. You would have to use a debt consolidation loan and will be charged interest – it could be easier to manage and more cost-effective.
5. **Order your debts:** Order your debts according to the debt repayment method you've chosen.
6. **Get started:** Make a budget, identifying what you want to achieve versus what you need and check all your spending (see Chapter 3). This will allow you to release some cash to start repaying some of your balances.

7. **Celebrate:** Share your new debt-free status with me, the Vestpod community and your friends and family.

Instead of paying off the minimum each month, you can also transfer the debt to a zero-interest card; look at the balance and see exactly how much you should repay to get the amount down to ZERO. However, be careful, as if you are feeling vulnerable to the money pressure, you could be tempted to access fast cash without examining the ever-more painful consequences (hello payday loans).

Stop paying fees!

Find out whether you are incurring overdraft fees, annual fees on your current account, monthly fees, bank transfer fees, fees on late payments, cash withdrawal fees (the worst – you will incur charges if you use your credit card to withdraw money) and credit card fees. Most of these are avoidable. Use a fee-tracking app to show you what you have been paying to your bank as well as unused subscriptions.

A bank account or a credit card that is in a healthy financial state should not be charging you for their services. If you think you have been charged bank charges unfairly (on an overdraft, for example) or if you have paid a monthly fee for your bank account, you can speak to your bank and ask them for a refund.

Who Can Help You?

Financial advisers

Financial advice is not just for the rich, and sometimes it is best to reach out to a professional and ask for help. You should never feel embarrassed or ashamed about doing so.

Financial advisers provide you with advice on how to manage money. They research the market and are able to offer financial products that will suit your personal financial situation, investment, retirement, insurance, etc.

YOU'RE NOT BROKE: YOU'RE PRE-RICH

The sector is carefully regulated and all financial advisers are listed and monitored by the FCA.

You can choose between two types of advisers depending on what area of personal finance you would like to focus on and get help with:

1. *Independent Financial Adviser (IFA):* IFAs provide impartial and unrestricted advice and are able to consider and recommend all types of retail investment products (i.e. pensions, investments) which could meet your needs and objectives. They work in your best interests and don't get paid commissions to push products.
2. *Restricted advisers:* These advisers can only offer limited advice. They focus on particular types of products and/or product providers (i.e. mortgage adviser, pension adviser, investment adviser, etc.) so it may be more difficult for you to understand what they can help you with. Advisers will typically provide advice on a product (*Do I need a pension or an ISA? Do I need insurance?*), but they should also provide you with broader comprehensive financial life planning (*Am I saving enough money? Will I have enough money to retire on? How can I achieve my goals?*). You will be able to discuss your financial goals, lifestyle and priorities and, based on this, they will work on a cash flow model and build a financial plan for you.

Do you need a financial adviser?

If you are young and have a financial life that is relatively simple (that is, you are not struggling with debt, you are single, you don't have kids, you don't have a large sum of capital to invest or you are just looking at saving money), you may not feel you need an adviser. For now, it may be enough just to manage to save some money and learn the basics about investing because the cost of financial advice can be prohibitive if you don't have a lot of money. As and when you embark upon more complex financial decisions and situations (planning for retirement, inheriting money) or major life transitions (buying a home, having a baby, getting married or perhaps divorced), you may want to get some more expert help.

Although financial advice will cost you some money, it will also in all likelihood save you time and provide you with knowledge that can add value to your future. According to Unbiased, people tend to save more in their pensions when taking independent financial advice.[11] If money is a source of stress, working with a professional could also boost your confidence.

What happens during a first meeting?

The first meeting with an adviser should always be free as it is a consultation. Do make sure that this is the case beforehand. The first session is usually called a 'fact-finding' meeting where the adviser can get to understand your goals, where you are today and how he or she can help you.

You will be asked about all the money taboos that you usually keep to yourself: how much you earn, save, have in your accounts, what are your assets, liabilities, etc. This can seem a little overwhelming (though if you have followed the advice in this chapter so far, you will be well-prepared).

The initial consultation is the best way to get to know an adviser. Focus on whether you think you could work with them on a personal level and whether they have helped you to form a better understanding of your goals and finances.

How to find an adviser

The ideal way to look for an advisor is via a personal recommendation from a friend, family member or colleague who has already worked with the adviser and is happy with their services.

If you can't find personal recommendations, there are many online directories. These sites list the advisers available near you and you can search for your specific needs. Always make sure that the advisers are qualified and listed by the regulator on the FCA website.

Once you have listed the subjects you would like to cover and the goals you would like to achieve, you can start to contact a handful of advisers by email or by phone. Some questions you can ask include:

- *Are you an independent (IFA) or restricted financial adviser?*
- *What certifications do you hold?*
- *What are the types of products you offer?*
- *Do you sell your own firm's financial products?*
- *How much will you charge for your services?*
- *How and when would I pay for them?*
- *What style of service will you provide: face-to-face/virtual meetings, calls, emails?*
- *What materials will I receive or what apps/software do you use?*

- *Can I see an example of a financial plan that you have prepared?*
- *Will I work with you exclusively or with someone else on your team?*
- *What is your experience as an adviser and what type of clients do you typically advise?*
- *How will you manage my investments? How often will we review these?*
- *What is your investment track record?*

Take time to read the small print and make sure you understand the services you will receive for the fees you will be paying. Make sure you meet them in person or via an online call before making any kind of decision.

How much does it cost?

According to a report by the FCA[12], there are two different charges made by advisers: the *initial charge*, which is for when you need specific advice as a one-off or first step of an ongoing process; and the *ongoing charge*, which is what you pay for the ongoing relationship with the adviser. Remember that the more advice you need, the more money it will cost you.

Financial coaching

It is important to note that financial guidance (or money coaching) is very different from financial advice (which comes from financial advisers). Financial advisers are regulated by the FCA and they will be able to recommend products for you. Financial coaches can't do that, they can only offer more generic information and help as a guide to navigating the personal finance landscape.

A good financial coach can help you rewrite your money narrative and methodology and teach you how to deal with the self-limiting beliefs and self-talk associated with money and earning potential, such as: 'I don't earn enough', 'I'm not worth it', 'I'll never have enough to live off', 'I will never clear my debts.'

Make sure you are happy with a financial coach's fees (which are usually fixed per hour) and credentials. Some can be ex-IFAs, while others may come from a non-financial background.

Beware of Scams!

It is important to know that your savings and any money deposited in an account have a level of protection, provided by the Financial Services Compensation Scheme (FSCS). If you live in the UK, always look for this on your provider's website or paperwork: 'Protected under the Financial Services Compensation Scheme (FSCS)'. That means that some of your money (up to a certain limit) is protected in this UK bank or building society, and you will get your money back if this bank fails. If you have more than the limit to save, spread it to another account in another bank for maximum protection. Visit the FSCS website to check current compensation limits.

Always remain vigilant because scammers are using newer and ever-smarter techniques to get at your identity and your money. They will usually approach you directly at home, by post/phone or email and will ask you for personal or login details. They will often offer you a deal too good to be true.

- Always keep your personal information confidential and protect your accounts with strong passwords that you change regularly.
- Check the company contacting you is legitimate on the FCA register website.
- Don't call a company back on the phone number they give you – get the number from the official website instead.
- Don't reply to text messages requiring urgent action. Instead, call the usual number you have on file.
- Check your bank statement for small withdrawals that seem unfamiliar. (Scammers will sometimes do a test transaction first.)
- Check your credit score online and look for unfamiliar applications.
- Make sure you switch to your mobile provider's data network instead of using public WiFi if you need to do an online bank transfer because these free WiFi spots have become prime targets for scammers and hackers.

If you've been scammed: Try to stop the payment and report the scam to Action Fraud.

If there is any chapter in this book worth rereading, it is this one, because in order to move forward, you need to understand your current financial status and recognise the money pitfalls that have tripped you up. This new understanding will serve as a foundation stone for the next stage of your pre-rich journey towards financial health and wealth – setting your money goals.

YOU'RE NOT BROKE: YOU'RE PRE-RICH

* *

CHAPTER 2

PLANNING FOR THE FUTURE

* *

What you will learn in this chapter:

How to put together a life plan

How to work on your financial goals

How to protect yourself and your family

* *

In this chapter, we will think about what your goals are and what you want to achieve in life, and explore some bigger ambitions. Thinking about these will offer you new ideas and guidance on how to fine-tune your own life goals to prioritize and achieve what you want.

We'll finish off the chapter by talking about protection so you can achieve your goals no matter what life throws at you.

Where Do You Want To Be?

Life will not necessarily turn out as we expect it to, but we need to aim for something and be prepared for the unexpected; once we reach our initial goal, we can then aim higher and bigger. Having a plan will allow you to achieve more, more quickly – especially when it comes to your finances.

Why do you need a plan?

We should all have a financial plan, and here is why:

To help you get to your destination and prevent procrastination

Knowing where you want to go might seem obvious, but sometimes the detail of how to reach your destination is not the first thing that springs to mind when you talk about your hopes and dreams. It can be tempting to put off making decisions, but your stress will compound (in a bad way) like the interest on a loan if you don't act now to put a financial plan in place.

To help you to become wealthier by saving more

If you want to be able to save more and build wealth over time, you will need to take smart financial decisions. Maybe you do this already but I can't emphasize enough that recognizing what you want versus what you need, having a better grip on your spending and saving small amounts of money over time will help you to grow your financial pot steadily.

To give you peace of mind and more confidence

By planning ahead for how much money you will need if you want to achieve your dreams, and by understanding what financial position you need to be in to buy a property, travel the world, start a family or retire early, you will develop a clear plan of action and find peace of mind.

To make you happy

According to a survey by Morningstar Financial Research, when people believe they can plan for their financial future and be in control of their money they feel better about money than those who have little control over their lives.[13]

To help you to sail through surprises

One of the major benefits of having a plan is that you can avoid unexpected situations and be in control, even when a bit of bad luck strikes and you need money urgently.

To force you to use numbers

Some of us can be reluctant to use the real numbers for planning purposes – but when you have a plan with actual figures you gain both clarity and confidence. And while financial advisers can produce in-depth plans for you with the help of software and algorithms, there are also many things you can start doing on your own.

To help you avoid ending up in debt

Building your own plan is the first step towards a debt-free life. You could also take this plan to an adviser later on to discuss how to fine-tune it. In these ways you can start looking ahead to a future where paying off debt becomes easier and doesn't ever lead to taking on more.

Write down your financial goals

Most of us have never done this exercise before and, at first, it can seem overwhelming, but try not to panic!

Ask yourself: Do I have an emergency fund? Do I have costly debts? Will I be making big purchases (house, cars, big birthday parties)? Do I want to change job or set up a business? Do I want to have children? Am I saving for retirement? Do I have to pay for my children's education, childcare and more? Do I plan to leave a legacy? Do I have insurances to protect myself? Will I have to support ageing parents? Do I have dreams?

Once you have a list of all the things you would like to achieve, break the time frame into four parts. It's always good to start today. As we've discussed, repaying our expensive debts, building up our emergency fund and making a budget are really key here!

1. **Today** (the next 1–2 years): Day-to-day spending, building emergency savings, repaying expensive debts?
2. **Short-term** (the next 2–5 years): Holidays, shopping, new laptop, car?
3. **Medium-term** (the next 5–10 years): Set up a business, deposit for a house, getting married?
4. **Long-term** (10 years+): Retirement, children's education?

To help you write down your goals, use the SMART approach:[14]
- **S**pecific: What exactly will you do with the money? What do you want to buy or what do you want to accomplish?
- **M**easurable: How much is the goal valued at? What is the exact amount (more or less)?
- **A**chievable: How can your goal be achieved? Is it realistic? Would a budget or spending plan help you to achieve it? Can you break down your goal into smaller goals to make it easier to achieve? What are the constraints?
- **R**elevant: Is your goal relevant? Does it motivate you? Is it meaningful enough? Can it challenge you?
- **T**imely: When do you want to achieve this goal by? If the horizon is too long and difficult to think about, can you create staged deadlines in between to help you to achieve things more quickly?

Without numbers and timelines, your goals are not realistic: it is hard to reach a goal if you don't know whether you're close to it or how to achieve it. Your goals have to be as closely connected as possible to your today and your current reality; creating a sense of urgency will help to achieve this! When a goal is vague and undetailed, it does not seem real. The less real it is, the less achievable it will be.

YOU'RE NOT BROKE: YOU'RE PRE-RICH

Visit vestpod.com/book to set your today, short-, medium- and long-term goals. You can then prioritise and rank them (some of them will be more urgent and important than others), to decide where you want to start first.

Once you have decided on your goals (with costs and timelines), create a game plan. How are you going to achieve this? What will it cost each month?

Take the measurable amount and divide by the number of years, then divide by 12, and you'll be left with the amount you need to save every month for each goal. Don't panic if the sum is greater than you expected. Think, is this realistic? Is it affordable? Maybe you could try to see if you could get there! If you see these goals are not yet reachable, revisit them and negotiate an achievable target.

Now, you can start working towards your goals, either simultaneously or according to the rank you gave them.

You should review your goals and update them regularly – the likelihood is that as you achieve some of your goals, others will start to seem outdated. Remember – you can always change your mind, your work and your life!

Stay accountable

This means that you and you alone are responsible for your actions and their consequences. Being accountable means not sweeping anything under the carpet and looking honestly at your every financial action, including Amazon orders, drunken internet shopping and giving money to charity. You have to own your transactions to make your money work for you.

Six ways you can stay accountable with your money
1. **Get a motto to live by:** Pick a phrase that is meaningful to you and prepare for the day ahead with it in the back of your mind. It might be something as big as 'achieve total independence' or as low-key as 'stay humble'.

2. **Find your tribe:** Whether it's a financial adviser, a friend, or even an online community like Vestpod, having the right person by your side can really help you to get things done.
3. **Use an app:** Online goal trackers or to-do-list apps are brilliant for helping you commit to your goal. You will be sent reminders when you need them, which will help you stay organised and focused.
4. **Visualize your goals:** Figure out your intentions and then focus, not necessarily on getting exactly what you want, but on connecting with the feeling of achieving your goal. Start by creating a mood board, whether on Pinterest or a physical version, with pictures associated with your goals.
5. **Break it down:** Set achievable targets and keep reviewing them to see how you're doing. If an item is still on your list after a month, it might not be something you're ever going to manage. If this is the case, scrap it!
6. **Reward yourself:** Once you've saved enough money, you can reward yourself with an educational experience like a fun cookery course, an investment class or a negotiation coaching session. Spending your hard-earned cash on an experience, rather than a commodity, will make a difference to the way you feel.

Prepare for a Family and Protect Them

If you decide to start a family, your life will become more complicated and your financial decisions will not just be about you anymore.

Preparing for coupledom

Imagine you've just got married or you've been dating your partner for some time. How do you manage your rent payments and day-to-day expenses? When is the right time for you to combine your finances? How do you both protect yourselves? Combining your finances is a big decision so think about the pros and cons:

Combine part of your finances:

- Open a new bank account under both your names and transfer a predetermined amount of money each month. The amount of money you transfer could be equal for both of you or calculated according to your income. The rest is kept in personal accounts.
- Combining your finances is a good way to help you track your expenses and keep on budget. You will need a new, shared and separate bank account to do this and it is a useful way to stash away the money needed for rent and bills at the beginning of the month. You'll have a better idea of where your money is going and how to keep a budget (as the expenses won't get mixed with your personal expenses).
- Bear in mind that you will both have full access to the account and that the money can be withdrawn by either of you at any time!

Keep it separate:

- Each has his/her own accounts.
- If you are not sure about combining your money or if it sounds a bit too much for you at this stage of your relationship, this may be your best option. Money is personal, and you need to feel in control and trust your partner with your money. This also works well for the long term.
- You can pay for household expenses by splitting them (use an app for that).

Combine everything:

- This involves receiving your income and managing a common current and saving account.
- Combining your finances is a big step. Whether it's for commitment, convenience or support, you need to agree with each other and set up some rules for what you can or cannot do. Before you take the plunge, ask each other honestly: do you have any debt? If yes, are you ready to share this debt?
- Make sure you protect your income and net worth. Sadly, many couples have to separate at some point or even divorce and this can become a tricky situation to manage (see page 42).

No one solution is better than another; these are very personal choices and often evolve with time.

TALK ABOUT MONEY WITH YOUR PARTNER

According to research by MoneyHelper, many people keep secrets from their partners: one in ten married UK adults has an 'escape fund' in case they want to leave; 13% have a 'secret stash of cash' that their spouse doesn't know about.[15] Even more shocking is that almost three in every ten adults in the UK have had a partner who they later found out was in serious debt.

You and your partner will have different money mindsets which are worth exploring individually – be objective and try to understand both of your behaviours and mindsets instead of casting judgement.

You need to discuss openly how you both spend money, what seems expensive to you both and how much money you want to earn. This can enable the trickier conversation surrounding how much you both earn.

Share knowledge: Knowing each other's salaries is key if you are to take shared financial decisions. Can you afford to buy a house or a car? Are you investing some money for the long term? Even if you decide to keep your finances separate, you have to understand how it works for the household, for your protection (does your partner have debts?) and for your choices (will you be able to live on one salary for the other to start a business, for example?).

Schedule time to talk: Find a time and place where you can be undisturbed for an hour – perhaps in a neutral space – then sit down together to look at your household spending. This offers time for you to raise concerns and brainstorm future financial plans.

Create a budget: Setting a budget really does take the stress out of your personal finance, and if you are setting the budget as a couple, you are sharing the load and the responsibility (and guilt if you break it).

> *Ask questions – and really listen to the answers:* If you feel annoyed
> or perplexed by your partner's spending habits, don't attack them.
> Try to understand where they have stemmed from. The overarching
> goal is to feel as though you're in this together: keep the channels of
> communication open and your finances will be healthier for it.

Preparing for a baby

It's no surprise that getting down to the nitty-gritty details of your family
finances may feel like the last thing you want to do with a new baby on the
scene, but whether you plan for your child's financial future pre- or post-
partum, it's something that simply has to be done. Here are four essential
considerations:

1. **Budget your maternity (and paternity) pay:** Reorganise your budget and
   start planning ahead for childcare costs. Decide for how long you will be
   off work and the maternity package in place – if any. When buying stuff
   for the baby, keep in mind that there are many items and products on the
   market that you really can do without, despite aggressive marketing to
   try to convince you otherwise!
2. **Life and health insurance:** If you haven't already got the former, it's time
   to strongly consider it (see page 39). And while health insurance isn't
   mandatory in the UK, if you or your partner is covered through a work
   scheme, you might want to add your child to your insurance plan, too.
3. **Make sure your will is up to date:** It may feel scary to think about, but
   writing/updating your will is likely to give you greater peace of mind.
   Besides the financial elements of your will, another vital thing to
   consider is who your child's guardian would be until they turn 18.
4. **Start saving for their future with a Junior ISA (Individual Savings Account)
   or a child pension – if you can:** Fasten your seatbelt first – your savings
   are a priority but if you can save more, there are cash or stocks and shares
   options for the junior ISA just as there are for the regular version (see
   page 82). But remember, you're not investing for yourself and won't be
   able to withdraw any of the money you put into a junior ISA. Only your
   child will be able to access their money, when they turn 18.

MOTHERHOOD PENALTY & CHILDCARE

Childcare is notoriously expensive. Families have to sit down and make calculations to determine whether or not it is worth a parent going back to work after having a child. Is there any financial incentive in returning to work while paying for childcare? You need to make a rational decision based on both of your salaries. If you are in the privileged position to be able to consider childcare, you should view it as an investment, not an expense. This may seem counter-intuitive, but taking into consideration the longer-term benefits of returning to work, such as the steady increase in salary and pension contributions, makes the process of paying for childcare a little less painful.

If you decide to stay at home for a few years and have no income, make sure you discuss with your partner whether they can top up your pension while you're not earning – it makes sense financially but is also a way to make the most of your tax allowances. And make sure you are claiming Child Benefit to qualify for NI credits.

Did you know that women who leave the workforce are penalized for doing so? An illuminating study distressingly revealed that women lose an average of 18% of their earning power if they take time out from the workplace for an average 2.2 years.[16] The more time you spend away from work, the bigger the reduction in salary when you return to work. After three years or more of being out of the workforce, the 18% reduction in earnings becomes a shocking 37%... It's quite a bitter pill to swallow!

Be Protected from the Unexpected

You can do all the planning in the world and have the most kick-ass dreams and achievements, but if something happens that is out of your control, it's a disaster. This is often referred to as 'a financial storm'.

YOU'RE NOT BROKE: YOU'RE PRE-RICH

Build an emergency fund

When the unexpected happens we are likely to throw money at the problem without thinking about the implications. But after paying out for that expensive laptop repair or medical costs incurred abroad, you can be left with a bill that's ruinous. The (simple) solution? Build your emergency fund.

Experts say that, as a good rule of thumb, you should aim to keep three to six months' living expenses to one side and that it should be possible to withdraw this money instantly (kept in an easy or instant access account); so make sure you hold the cash in a savings account you can access. Living expenses are basically the cost of living: your rent or mortgage, food, groceries, utilities, debt, basic needs.

If you're thinking *'What?! That sounds crazy. How am I supposed to save that much money?'* then create a plan. As for any goal, you need to start somewhere. Stash small amounts every month and increase how much you save gradually. Over time, you'll reach your goal and have this rainy day fund that you can fall back on in time of need.

Insurance

Life insurance (also known as life cover and death cover)

No one likes to think about life insurance, much less talk about it or buy it. But it's important to be pragmatic when it comes to taking care of your loved ones, and life insurance could make all the difference to their future. To determine whether you need it, ask yourself two key questions:

1. Do you have dependants?
2. Would they suffer financially if you weren't around to provide for them?

Life insurance is a way of paying an income or lump sum to your family if you die. It's for people who are major breadwinners in a family group. If your income is important for paying the mortgage, school fees or general expenses, insurance could give you some peace of mind. Always bear in mind that the cost of the insurance will depend on your age and your current health.

Many employers offer life insurance to their employees as part of a benefits package. If your employer doesn't offer life insurance, you should take a look at other options:

- Consult with a financial adviser to get some help to find the best cover for you. Insurance brokers could also help you out.
- Visit comparison websites to learn more about different types of cover and find something that works best for you and your family.

Income protection insurance

This provides you with some cover if you can't earn an income because you are unable to work due to a serious illness or injury, usually until you return to paid work or you retire.

Critical illness insurance

Critical illness insurance is a long-term insurance policy that protects you and pays you a tax-free lump sum on diagnosis of a specific illness or injury listed in the policy. The cash benefit can help you to pay off your mortgage or debts, or pay for additional medical help, but it's up to you how you spend it.

House insurance

This one is mandatory if you own a property. If you have a mortgage in place, the mortgage provider would have required you to subscribe to a building insurance, so that in the case of something happening (fire, massive cracks, etc.), you are covered. However, you will still have to pay for your own repairs or a new boiler. You can also add contents insurance, which will cover anything you lose in case of one of the above events, or if you are burgled.

Health insurance (also called Private Medical Insurance/ PMI)

While you may not see it as a necessity, PMI is sometimes an important thing to have. Some form of medical cover may also be included in your work benefits, so make sure you check what you have. There are different types of cover available, from basic (access to a GP and referrals to specialists) to Gold plans (including dental care and private clinic birth delivery). Bear in mind that some cheaper plans don't cover in-patient treatment so if you ever require a stay in hospital following surgery or an accident then you won't be covered privately.

Private health insurance can be quite costly. You have a monthly or annual premium that you pay upfront and there is also an excess (a certain amount you pay towards your medical bills before any repayment kicks in). The larger the excess paid for, the lower the premium.

Car insurance

If you have a car, you need car insurance. There are three levels of protection you can choose from that will also have different price points (called premiums) from low to high: from the basic 'Third party' (protecting you against damage that's caused by you to others), to 'Third party, fire and theft' (same as previous but with extra protection: they will replace your car if stolen or damaged/destroyed by fire) and 'Comprehensive car insurance' (most things covered). The price you pay is determined by a lot of things including driving/accidents history, personal circumstances, car, parking, etc. Head over to comparison websites and see what they offer.

Travel insurance

Travel insurance protects you from painful and expensive risks such as cancelled flights, ski injuries, lost luggage and much more. Make sure you read the small print in the terms and conditions. If you have a credit card, it's possible it includes travel insurance.

If you need help, why not check with your bank or insurance broker?

What's your legacy?

Personal finances are of course about us, but how do you protect your loved ones and leave a legacy? While I can't tell you what is exactly right for you, there are a few things we can review that should help you understand the bigger picture. You should definitely consult an adviser for this exercise too!

Do you have a will?

Financial advisers unanimously agree that writing a will is vitally important; it gives you the power to decide what happens to your money, property and possessions after you die, and helps protect the lives of loved ones that you leave behind. When there is no will in place, some rules automatically apply to divide the assets. These are called the rules of intestacy.[17] So it is imperative to get it done and dusted – regardless of your age, health or the state of your finances.

Nominate someone for your pension

When you die, your pension will be left to your beneficiary (the person who inherits it) and pensions are normally (but not always) exempt from inheritance tax. Make sure you review this area and inform your pension provider of who your beneficiary should be – it can be anyone. This is a complex area and you may want to speak to an adviser to understand tax implications.

What if you can't decide for yourself?

If you are well and in full command of your affairs but fear that might change due to illness or accident, you can nominate a friend or family member to take over your affairs if or when you are no longer able to carry on. They will be allowed to make healthcare and financial decisions and transactions on your behalf. A Lasting Power of Attorney (LPA) should give you and your loved ones peace of mind, because without it people can't take decisions for you.

Inheritance rules – make the most of them

The government will tax the estate (assets) that you leave behind when you die (cash, property, investments, insurance pay-outs and so on) minus your debts. Inheritance tax (IHT) is payable on possessions that are passed on when you die, above a certain tax threshold.

Make sure you check the rules on the government website to see how much you can give away before paying tax.[18] Note that when you leave some of your money to charity, you can also reduce the taxes you pay.

Getting married: protecting each other

I have met many women who have committed to their partner, mixed up their finances and debt with them, and ended up in a very difficult financial situation – having to bear the debts of the other party after they have split up. To avoid this, plan ahead to make sure you are 100% certain of everything you sign up to and the consequences it may cause. Get advice, talk about it.

Even if you're a die-hard romantic, you can't deny the importance of a prenuptial agreement. A prenup is a written document agreed by both partners before their wedding. It sets out the possessions of each as well as how things should be split in case of divorce. It can be quite flexible, and it can also be revisited after the wedding. If worst comes to worst and you decide to go your separate ways, a prenup will help ease what will already be a painful and complicated time.

In the UK, courts recognize prenuptial agreements, but they can also have their view and waive it if they feel it is unfair or if you have children. So, while it is useful, judges may overrule it to look at the financial needs of both parties.

In the case of a divorce, you need to get advice, rather than trying to sort things out yourself – it's a complicated area and having extra moral support will help you through the difficult process. What if you can't talk to each other? What if you discover too late that your partner has bad debts? What if you end up with a lot of money that you have absolutely no clue to manage? What if you don't work and your partner was the breadwinner? There is a multitude of questions that could arise, so prepare and protect yourself the best you can.

Go to the government website if you need more info on money and divorce.[19]

With so much thinking and learning under your belt, it is hopefully safe to say that you now have a plan in place. You've figured out what your real goals are and *the type of life you would like to live*. Better still, by now you should understand the basics of how to protect your assets from the vicissitudes that life might throw at you. It can be quite overwhelming to know all these but, step by step, you'll start implementing what's important to you and make sure you are better prepared for life!

Be open to things changing and factor frequent check-ins into your plan. Remember – change and self-awareness are good, and they are what this process is all about.

* *

CHAPTER 3
OWN IT: GET A GRIP ON YOUR MONEY

* *

What you will learn in this chapter:
How to make a spending plan (aka set a budget)
How to get a better understanding of the way you spend money
How to cut costs and release some money each month

* *

The secret to having personal wealth is knowing where your money is going – every week and every month – because understanding your outgoings allows you to form new money habits and start to save. This chapter is going to help you take a non-judgemental look at your spending decisions. This does not need to be painful – we won't be making any grand plans to begin with, just small, smart hacks, with a sprinkling of what it means to transition into being a saver.

Where is All Your Money Going?

The first step towards getting real is to take action today. Confront your spending, start to examine where your money is going and focus on breaking your negative thought patterns. Developing clarity and a firm understanding of where you stand financially will help you achieve your goals. To help with this we need to look at two things: financial planning (with the help of a budget) and understanding your spending decisions.

In theory, building wealth is a simple process, but it takes time and consistency to achieve in practice. The basic principle is to spend less than you earn each month, in order to save. To achieve this, you need to wise up to differences between wasteful spending and smart spending.

Do you want it or do you need it?

Analysing your spending behaviour can help you achieve self-knowledge, and with that comes the ability to be kinder to yourself when you slip up (though the slip-ups will happen less as self-awareness grows). Looking closely at what you spend will also gradually change your money mindset and enable you to start spending in a way that feels more purposeful.

Think about your latest big financial decision and ask yourself these questions:

What triggered your wish to buy this?

Why did you decide to buy it?

Did it make you happy and why?

For how long did it make you happy?

What did you have to give up to be able to afford to buy it? Was it the cheapest option available? Why?

This process of cross-examination will help you to assess which things you want and which you need. There is scope for both wants and needs in your budget, but obviously needs have to be prioritized.

What are your needs?

Essentially, financial needs are requirements for you to be able to live and work. They probably include: housing costs (including rent or mortgages, bills and maintenance), groceries, transportation, communication – the internet and a phone – clothes and insurances and debt repayments.

What are your wants?

Wants are the things you buy that are not essential but will give you a more comfortable life. These would include travel, entertainment, shopping, dining out, etc. If you take a look at all the things you bought (or wanted to buy) last month, you will probably find that you convinced yourself you 'needed' most of them. However, if you think carefully about each item you spend money on, you may come to a deeper understanding of what you really want and need.

Budgeting Guidelines

Budgeting is the process of creating a plan to manage and spend your money. There are many different ways to set a budget. However, there is one formula that underlines all of the basics of budgeting:

Understanding what comes in (+) and goes out (-) of your pocket each week, each month and each year = more money

Living to a budget may not feel sexy but it is essential. If we don't know how much we are making or how much we are spending, how can we ever start to think about saving money or investing money? Being in control of your finances is truly liberating. Setting a budget makes saying 'no' to yourself a great deal easier.

The 50/20/30 budgeting goal

The 50/20/30 budgeting guideline was first introduced by the Harvard bankruptcy expert Elizabeth Warren and her daughter, Amelia Warren Tyagi.[20] (It was known initially as the 50/30/20 rule.)

50/20/30 is also called percentage or proportional budgeting. 50/20/30 means that 50% of your income is allocated to essential expenses, 20% to financial goals, and the remaining 30% to lifestyle (aka flexible spending). The order is important here and that's why we address the 50% first then the 20% and finish with the 30%. By working first on your needs and directly after that on your savings goals you substantially increase your ability to save – instead of waiting to see what's left at the end of the month...

This budgeting goal is empowering and effective because it is not as stringent as the typical method of counting every pound that goes in and out of your pocket. It is a simple and very adaptable guide to how you should allocate your money. If you have a fluctuating income, you can look at the average of the last three to six months rather than monthly.

You can decide to apply this budgeting goal to your salary pre- or post-pension contribution figure. Just be consistent when you do your calculation over time. If you are a freelancer or a contractor you will need to calculate this yourself: work out how much you earn and then subtract the taxes you are expected to pay. You can also use a net salary calculator on the internet, which is a pretty nifty way to get started.

50%: The 50% category comprises of all your 'essential expenses':

- *rent or mortgage payments*
- *utilities: electricity, water and gas*
- *groceries*
- *transport*
- *mobile phone and internet*
- *debt payments*

Although the headline figure is 50%, for some people the percentage will be higher as they will need to pay more for rent, transport and so on. It's important to note that the ratios have to be adjusted to work for your life – they're just an indication but you should set your own targets.

20%: The 20% category – 'pay yourself first' – is money you will be putting towards your financial goals and savings, for example:

- *Paying back extra debt if you are trying to get debt-free.*
- *Building an emergency or rainy-day fund (see page 39).*
- *Saving for your short- to medium-term goals (the ones you worked on in Chapter 2).*
- *Saving for your long-term goals (retirement funds and pensions).*

Don't try to reach the 20% saving goal if you can't afford it – you can start with a lower number and have a percentage goal in mind for the future – the most important goal is to get started, and to develop the habit of saving some money. If saving too much will put you in the red at the end of the month, reduce your saving goal – there is no point borrowing on your credit card to increase your savings.

30%: The 30% spending category is the 'wants' we talked about earlier and includes your lifestyle choices. What is left from your income is your guilt-free spending pocket. Whether you are a shopaholic or a foodie, your 30% lifestyle spending can cover a range of things – but you may consider some of these things essentials:

- *charity donations and gifts for your loved ones and friends*
- *TV and online entertainment*
- *shopping*
- *sport and gym subscriptions*
- *entertainment*
- *eating out*
- *travel*
- *personal development*
- *beauty treatments*

The 50/20/30 Bugeting goal

EXERCISE

Grab your money notebook, open an Excel file or go to vestpod.com/book to build your own budgeting goal inspired by 50/20/30. For this exercise, you will need to have your last three bank statements to hand and be ready to look into all your numbers.

• Based on previous months, determine your current percentages (essentials, pay yourself and lifestyle).

• Now based on your goals and how much you think you can save, what is your new allocation?

The envelope system

This budgeting method uses only cash – that is physical cash in physical envelopes! With the envelope system you withdraw the money you need each week and put it into the corresponding envelopes. For example, envelopes labelled 'rent', 'savings', 'healthcare', 'kids', 'gym', 'clothing', 'transport' and so on. The good news is that this back-to-basics accounting system has been made digital, so you can apply the envelope system to your cash without using physical cash.

The reason this simple system is so useful is because it stops you overspending or feeling guilty about spending, and ensures you stick to a budget.

Zero-sum based budget

With a zero-based budget, all your income is used to cover all of your outgoings, including savings, so you end up with zero at the end of the month. This method is useful if you overspend each month and, for example, always end up with additional expenses on your credit card.

In the end, your best option is to learn about and research the different budgeting methods available and decide what feels right, what suits your money (and spending) style and what you think you will be able to stick to. You could also create your own approach by taking some inspiration from these basic methods.

How to Spend Money Wisely

It's OK to spend money! But it's also important to recognise that emotions will influence the way you think and behave with money.

'Emotional spending' or 'retail therapy' happens when we're trying to change our mood (bored, anxious, lonely, unhappy) – we're seeking instant gratification and the 'shopper's high'[21] from dopamine, one of the brain's neurotransmitters – but, unfortunately, this uncontrollable spending can have disastrous effects on our finances.

Control emotional spending

We all enjoy a little retail therapy but it becomes a worry when things start getting out of control and we don't realise we're overspending or we lose control of how much money we're spending.

If you want to change this habit, start by thinking about why you make certain financial choices, and what the triggers and emotions are that make you purchase these items in the first place. For me, the key is to understand that I shouldn't buy something just because I can afford it – there's so much value in switching to a more sustainable approach to shopping.

Another angle is to stop making treats 'forbidden' by tweaking your budget. Factor in a monthly amount for impulse spending and prepare lists of the things you want to buy. Now it's time to set a monthly shopping date and get ready for it with a determined budget. Who knows, once you know that you are allowed to spend money on a so-called bargain, you might even decide that you don't want to.

You could also try following the 10/10 rule: if an item costs more than £10, spend 10 minutes thinking about it. If after that time you're still not sure whether to buy it, put it back on the shelf or leave it in your online basket for a little longer. That should save you some time and money![22]

The most effective hack works at a deeper psychological level. Start becoming aware of 'opportunity cost': this means pausing before you spend to ask yourself what future benefit you might lose out on if you spend unbudgeted money on an unplanned purchase right now. When you say no to that pair of shoes, don't see your decision as a sacrifice, instead see it as a great opportunity to make your true goals happen more quickly! This is called delayed gratification.

Another reason we fall for the lure of an impulse buy is because they are marketed boldly. They may flash up on a web page with a big red banner saying 'Last chance to buy!' or be strategically positioned by a checkout queue in a high-street store. Arm yourself against merchandisers' tricks by telling yourself that you are not scoring a cool, cut-price treat, but falling into a trap laid by a ruthless advertiser.

Spend money on experiences vs. material goods

Thomas Gilovich, a psychology professor at Cornell University, says that, in order to achieve longer-term happiness, we should spend money on experiences rather than things.[23]

It is important to remember that happiness isn't just one fleeting moment of satisfaction – it is something that needs to be measured and sustained over time, and that in the pre-rich mindset, it is our experiences, not our possessions, that create greater longer-term happiness.

Spend money with your values

Your values today may (or may not) be different tomorrow. You may value travel, achievement, education and hard work today, but move towards family, adventure, security and equality tomorrow. They will change as you grow, but it is essential to hold them at the forefront of your mind. Try to understand what you value in life. You can write your values down today in order to establish what presently makes you happier, but ensure that you come back to the list every year at least and reflect upon them.

Frugality: less is more

Frugality is not being stingy but making sure you don't overconsume. Whether rich or poor, people are wising up to the fact that spending money they have or do not have on shiny stuff they do not need may not be making them happy in the long run. Look around you and take note of all the stuff you already own. Doesn't it already meet your needs pretty well? If it is not useful or doesn't bring you satisfaction, start decluttering – you'll feel lighter for it.

Give money

Try to think back to the last time you gave something away – perhaps a donation or a gift to someone in need. How did it make you feel? Scientists are finding that the brain is hardwired for generosity and a study by professors Elizabeth Dunn, Lara Aknin and Michael Norton highlights a direct correlation between giving and feeling happy.[24]

Being altruistic also promotes social recognition and connection: sociologists Brent Simpson and Robb Willer have suggested that your generosity is likely to be rewarded by others down the line – a little thing we like to call *good karma*.[25]

Your time has value too

You are used to asking yourself 'Where has all my cash gone?' or 'How do I spend my money?', but it is time to start asking yourself the same questions about what you do with your time too. This can apply to business owners and managers as much as individuals, because we all need to question what we are spending most of our time on. Is it valuable and useful and contributing to our goals, or is it wasteful and pointless in the long run? The crux of it is that our goals are usually more to do with personal freedom than the amounts of money involved.

Can you ask yourself: What makes you happy? How much does it cost? Can you do more of it?

Saving Tips and Tricks

Remember, small steps compound over time!

Be smart with your bills

Set a morning aside to phone each of your utilities providers and ask them how you could cut your bills. Use an online comparison website to find the best deal for you and your wallet and don't hesitate to switch supplier.

Turn off the tap

The easiest way to reduce your water bill is to reduce your water consumption. If you pay a fixed rate for your water bills, you should look into getting a water meter.

Pay attention to your mobile and broadband

Double-check your broadband and mobile plans, as well as your bills – it is highly likely that you are paying too much for your plan, including extra costs. Call your provider and ask for a better deal, but do your research beforehand and switch if you find a better rate elsewhere.

Shop like a pro

Use your common sense and don't get sucked in by chance-of-a-lifetime deals: they are nearly always designed to make more money for the vendor. However, when you know you need to buy something, make sure you browse online for the best discounts.

Be aware of anchoring

Anchoring is a trick used by marketers to get the purchaser to compare prices, rather than reflect on the true value of what they are buying. So, when a price is first thrown at you, you might react with, 'Wow that is super high!' You are then offered a lower price, so you compare the prices and think that you have scooped a great deal. But did you even want to buy the item in the first place?

Cancel your subscriptions

Recent research found that 65% of homes are signed up to regular subscriptions services with an average of seven per household, making the UK a 'subscription society'![26] Make sure you review and cancel your unwanted subscriptions using an app.

Embrace sustainable shopping

Buying new essentials is always tempting but their value decreases as soon as you have paid for them. By shopping more sustainably, on top of the obvious savings, you are also helping to save the planet by recycling and preventing waste. Could you get what you want second-hand instead? Or rent it out? Start browsing second-hand marketplaces online. You can use your creativity to give new life to goods that would have been wasted and even resell them after you've used them too (upcycling), with a much lower depreciation.

Make your wardrobe pay your bills

Raise your hand if you own at least one article of clothing that you've only ever worn once. Yeah – that's literally everybody reading this. The good news is that one person's ill-fitting get-up is another person's treasure, so why not free up space in your wardrobe and monetize your blunders using second-hand retailers such as: eBay, Vestiaire Collective, Vinted or DePop?

Prepare a weekly meal plan

Those £10 takeaway lunches. Seriously? £10 x 20 working days is already £200! We won't even talk about the health side of it. Plan your meals ahead of time, shop according to your list, prepare them on Sunday (batch cooking) and store them in the fridge of freezer. Follow some foodies on social media for inspiration; you'll save money and time, too!

Keep an eye on your food deliveries

How easy has it become to order food directly from your sofa without moving a muscle? Check your delivery apps and see how much you have been spending per month recently. Set a budget for it!

Say no to 'witching hour' and impulse shopping

According to a report by Barclaycard, 'One in three Brits now spends more money shopping online at night, compared to five years ago.'[27] So make sure you stop browsing past 8pm or only add to your basket – don't check out at the risk of regretting it the next day. A good trick is to delete your card details from retailers' websites, disable the one-click payment option and turn on instant banking notifications on your phone.

Avoid sneaky add-ons

Temptation is everywhere... When something is on offer as a cheap add-on purchase, don't buy it and try to click 'next' without even looking at the retailer 'before you go' recommendations. Also unsubscribe from impulse buying triggers (email marketing).

Same-day delivery is clocking up your costs

Does your delivery driver know you personally or do you get excited when the doorbell rings with a delivery? That's maybe a sign that you're becoming addicted to online shopping. Think more sustainably, allow time for your parcels to arrive and group your order – you may realise you don't even need these items.

Check your council tax

According to MoneyHelper, up to 400,000 households have been assigned the wrong council tax band.[28] It only takes a few minutes to check your status and appeal an incorrect amount. Check out your local council's website. You can also follow the step-by-step guide found on the MoneySavingExpert website.[29]

These are small, easy things you can start today that can make a big difference. Over time, they should help you spend less and save more for your goals – whether or not you're ready to get started budgeting. This was one part of the equation: spending better and saving more. Next we will move on the second part: earning more!

* *

CHAPTER 4
ASKING FOR MORE MONEY

* *

What you will learn in this chapter:
How much you should be earning
How to negotiate your salary or rates
How to make extra money and build a business

* *

It's time to look reality in the eye and start to take some of the emotional and social shame out of asking for more money. Earning more is not the sole goal: earning more coupled with managing this money and keeping expenses under control will help you to save money – and saving money is the secret to building wealth.

If you stay organized and realistic, you could also make extra income by combining an employed role with freelance work or a side project. There are so many options out there!

How Much Should You Be Earning?

Understanding how much we need to live on is really helpful to avoid living pay cheque to pay cheque. This might sound like the preserve of the low paid, but high-earning millennials are the worst hit by the cycle of having nothing left at the end of each month.

How much do you need to earn?

It's useful to start by asking yourself these two questions:

1. 'How much do I need to earn to live and achieve my goals?'
2. 'How much do I need to earn to live comfortably or extravagantly?'

This exercise is pretty straightforward if you are an employee but not if you are a freelancer or self-employed. So do keep reading!

Extra tips for freelancers

The revenue you make as a freelancer can be unpredictable and cash flow can be precarious, and you also don't get the benefits associated with a job (think health insurance, workplace pension and perks).

If you are not employed but self-employed, you can contribute to a pension plan and you get the tax relief from the government, but you don't have an employer to financially support you. Also, remember that paid holiday leave isn't included. You usually get paid per day or hour of work so be sure to divide this number by the number of days you are planning to work per year.

The reality for freelancers is you don't spend 100% of your time 'billing' clients – there are times when you need to update your portfolios, market yourself, meet prospective clients, learn new skills, go to conferences, prepare invoices, and much more, which can take up to one day a week (20% of your time) and so should also be discounted from the days worked.

Freelancers, here is how to calculate your rates:

How much do I need to live comfortably?	£
Add up expenses	£
Add up medical insurance	£
Add up pension contribution	£
Your number	£
Divide by the number of hours you will be working – 20%	£

How much are you worth?

The workplace is a competitive arena and, as with anything worth fighting for in life, it helps to have the skills and confidence to show bosses and clients why we deserve both advancement and better pay.

Here are some tactics to help take stock of your true worth at work:

- Do your *research* to understand how much someone in a similar position and with similar experience earns elsewhere.
  - Because money is that much of a taboo, it can be hard to have a direct conversation with your peers, so start online. You can use the online salary tools from GlassDoor, PayScale or LinkedIn. They collect millions

of data and are helpful as a guide to allow you to search and fine-tune your salary expectations by location, skills and level of experience. Using these platforms will allow you to have hard numbers to hand, ready for any negotiation. (Though always take the findings with a pinch of salt if you work in a niche sector or in an industry that does not reveal salaries, such as banking.)

o If you are a freelancer, finding out the going rates may be harder, but still very much possible. Speaking to other freelancers doing the same job can prove useful in terms of finding out about rates, but also helpful in understanding how other people price their services. By asking for more you also increase the value of your work for others.

o Another way to stay updated with the market and understand how much people like you could be earning is to keep in touch with *recruiters and headhunters*. They hold a lot of information on levels of salaries for a certain industry and expertise.

o It's OK to talk about salary and sometimes necessary; the secrecy around pay is detrimental to achieving equality. According to the Equality Act of 2010, you can discuss your salary if you think you're being underpaid.[30]

- Get *another offer* somewhere else. Even if you aren't ready to leave your current position, another offer can give you the extra confidence and negotiating power you need. By keeping abreast of the job market you also stay aware of skills, your employability and companies that are hiring. Often the best way to get a raise is to move to another company. Don't undervalue the power of negotiating a first offer because, once you've got the job, that may be much harder. Another idea could be to look at switching industries, gain more knowledge and skills, go back to school for additional training in a field that appeals to you, or accept an entry-level job and learn as you go.

- *Keep calm.* During this process you might well discover that your colleague makes 20% more than you do. This is infuriating but it's also a good opportunity to ask for more.

Getting Paid: Employees

It may help to have a copy of your payslip to hand while reading through this section! Your payslip must show the following information: gross pay (full pay before any deductions), net pay (pay after deductions) also called 'take home' pay – this is the number that we usually look at first; and all other deductions (variable costs, such as NI contributions, and fixed costs: expenses you have incurred that your employer agrees to pay for). Your payslip also notes how your salary is paid to you – often via BACS.

Your payslip also includes information that is not mandatory such as your tax code (this code provided by HMRC will tell your employer how much tax they should deduct from your salary) and your *NI number* (this number is unique to you. You will keep it forever and it will help HMRC to understand how much you have been earning and paying in taxes).

You should check with your employer that they have the right details. A wrong tax code means that you may not be paying the right amount of tax and you could be overpaying (or worse, underpaying).

On your payslip you can also look at your earnings, deductions and pension.

HOW IS INCOME TAX CALCULATED?

When you earn money, you are required to pay taxes. However, there is an annual income threshold, below which you do not have to pay any tax. This is called the 'personal allowance'.

You pay taxes on any amount earned that is more than the personal allowance, as a percentage of your income, based on incremental bands. Different percentages are payable, according to certain thresholds. Make sure you check HMRC's website for the current rules.

If you are paying money towards a workplace pension, you will see this on your payslip. This is not a deduction but a contribution. If your employer is contributing too, you may also be able to see their balance on your payslip. Otherwise you can check your pension statements for more detail. (For more on workplace pensions, head to Chapter 5.)

If you're *repaying a student loan*, it will also appear on your payslip. Your employer is responsible for collecting the money due, directly from your salary, and will send it to the Student Loans Company to repay part of your loan.

Making a Living Out of a Freelancing Career

Many people dream about freelancing: think less commuting, more time with your family and greater control over what your day looks like... Freelancing is getting more popular and this is especially true among women. But what does freelance life really look like?

It should go without saying, but before taking the plunge to go freelance, take an honest look at what you have to offer. If you have the skill set and the determination to make freelancing work, then you're starting from the right place. Freelancing is hard work and rewarding but also lonely at times. While you don't have a boss anymore, you have something that can be more challenging: clients. Freelancers have an entrepreneurial mindset, they set their own rules and drive their businesses. They bear their own risk whereas employees have stability.

How can you make sure you will be able to pay your bills at the end of each month? If your clients were to 'forget to pay you' for a few weeks or months, ask yourself, 'Can I survive financially?' The first rule of thumb is to make sure you have a cash surplus available in case of need. This is the all-important emergency fund and short-term savings I mentioned on page 39.

Getting paid

As a freelancer, one of the first but trickiest things you have to do is decide how much to charge:

- Start with a rate that will allow you to live comfortably and save towards your financial goals.
- Go online and seek out chat boards for your industry, where other freelancers are discussing what they get paid.
- Join a network of small business owners or freelancers such as The Dots to share best practices and rates.
- Ask your prospective client what their budget is, and what they usually pay (then check, if you can, with another freelancer or client whether this is true!).

YOU'RE NOT BROKE: YOU'RE PRE-RICH

You can choose to charge by the day (or hour) or for the whole project. Most businesses use the pay-by-time model because it's more straightforward for everyone involved. Knowing how much you're being paid per day will make your budgeting a whole lot easier too.

Paying taxes

If you have decided to go freelance or set up your own business, you will need to think about your business structure (sole trader, partnership or private limited company) and pay your own taxes (income tax, VAT, corporation tax) and NI contributions. When you are self-employed you pay taxes on your profits: income minus your business expenses.

As soon as you start working for yourself or receive income from your company you need to register as self-employed. This means registering for Self Assessment with HMRC to pay tax and NI contributions on your self-employed earnings. Working as self-employed requires you to be extra careful with your financial planning because you will earn money first and pay tax later. It is vitally important that you put money aside for this!

What about a pension?

If you are self-employed you won't receive a workplace pension, so it is your own responsibility to set up and contribute into a private pension (see Chapters 5 and 6). If you earn more than the basic rate, you will have to ask for your additional tax relief through your Self Assessment tax return. If you have your own business you could get tax advantages through your pension too.

Sort out your accounting

Whatever your business status you need to keep records of what's coming in and out, the sales you are making and the costs. As your business grows you will also need to consider payroll and office space costs.

There are online accounting packages and solutions you can use, such as xero.com or sage.com, that could save you time and keep you organized, but your best investment is to find an accountant who can help you to plan ahead, prepare your accounts if needed and budget accurately for your taxes.

Visit the government website for business and self-employed advice.[31] Don't hesitate to also give them a call as they are pretty responsive.

Learn new skills

Enriching your portfolio with an ever-expanding skill set can help increase your market value. Keep learning new computer programs, languages, accounting practices, communications techniques. And tell people about those skills!

Be creative

Don't stick to one way of finding work or just one set of clients. There could be a great project out there for you in the most unexpected place, so keep your eyes and mind open and don't automatically discount any potential offer that comes your way.

How to Negotiate

Negotiating is one of the key skills we need to grow. It requires a positive mindset and a willingness to improve things. It's important to be clear about what you want to get out of a negotiation and work hard to achieve it without losing out or becoming aggressive; some things are worth fighting for, but others less so. The best kinds of negotiation are always 'win-win' (so that all parties feel happy with the outcome) rather than 'win-lose'. There is almost always middle ground to be found.

The tactics discussed below on salary negotiation also apply to freelancing because you need to negotiate your rates.

Earn it!

This may be the most important 'detail' needed before starting any salary negotiation or rate increase. To earn more you have to first have earned it! If you know you are not genuinely giving 100%, you may feel less inclined to push for a promotion or salary/rate increase. When you know that you can demonstrate your true value, you will, in turn, feel more confident about asking for more. So, make sure you're truly giving it your all before you go in all guns blazin'...

Build your case

Based on how much you think you're worth, can you prepare a simple case to support your negotiation? How much do you earn today? How much do you want to earn tomorrow, and what are you basing this on? What are your targets? How will you achieve them? What will that bring to the table? What are your strengths? Based on this, it is useful to start any negotiation with three numbers in mind (i.e. on paper) – these will be your negotiation range. These numbers are for you and should not be seen by your employer/client, or prospective employer/client. You should ask yourself:

- *What is your current salary/rate? Is it at the market rate? Does it cover your budget and financial goals?*
- *What is the lowest salary/rate you can accept (the base rate – i.e. the amount of money you would accept for the job that will help you cover your needs and wants)? Make sure this level helps you to work towards your goals, is fair and is in line with the market.*
- *What is the ideal salary/rate you're aiming for? This amount should allow you to live comfortably and achieve your financial goals a bit quicker, but should also make sure you are paid what you're worth, i.e. the market value.*

Based on this, write down your three numbers.

- ....

- ....

- ....

Note your achievements and successes

Take notes on a weekly basis of all the things you do in your role: perhaps you bring new business to the firm, consistently reach targets, are great at networking, presentations, deals, new hires, management... Take note of any positive feedback you have received from management, clients and peers that links to your role and responsibilities. Prepare a business case that details successful KPI data (Key Performance Indicators: the number of new clients on board, number of deals signed, number of hours billed and so on; you should know the ones that are used to measure your performance) as well as changes in your role and responsibilities. Keeping track of your productivity will be instrumental in promoting your value and help others to recognize your worth both internally and externally. It's also very empowering to see what you've achieved, and we should all do this regularly, regardless of current negotiations!

When meeting prospective clients, freelancers are usually asked to provide a portfolio of their work, so get that looking sharp in advance. Your portfolio, just like a CV, should include client names, testimonials and case studies. Be specific about showing the value you have brought to past clients, even if it feels as if you are spelling out the obvious. Pitching for work is a sales job so it's important for you to start showing off those skills.

Find your supporters

We are not always comfortable negotiating for ourselves. A study by the American Psychological Association (via *Harvard Business Review*) shows that women usually negotiate better for others than for themselves; they are great advocates.[32] So, try to find colleagues/clients/peers who can champion you. Can you be more sociable at work and make more time for coffee catch-ups?

Your network is extremely valuable, so take every opportunity to socialize and work with a broad range of your industry fellows. Also think about mentorship, coaching or having a group of personal advisers outside of work that can support you and give you regular advice.

Don't accept the first offer

Congrats on getting a job offer or a salary/rate increase but remember, you don't have to accept it on the spot. I suggest asking for one or two days to think about it; then come back with a new proposal or counter-offer if you think it is necessary. Remember, too, that if someone asks you what amount you are looking for, you also don't have to state a precise figure for the salary/rate you want. Some people find it easier to state a range; you could also let your employer/client make the first offer, which could give you a good basis for negotiation. It is important that your employer/client feels comfortable with the level they are willing to offer.

Stay true to yourself

Authenticity is key to successful negotiations. Be your strong, open, true self. Value your skills and have faith in knowing the great things you have to bring to the company/client.

Put yourself in their shoes

Spend some time thinking about your request from the other person's perspective. If you feel as if you are being undervalued, why do you think that is? Perhaps they haven't noticed the extra time you have put in, or your commitment to your role or the company. Demonstrate your value the next time you're in a meeting with management/your client. If you focus on the added value you provide, they will start to think about you in terms of increasing the bottom line of the business and be more likely to agree to your request. Another simple hack is to use the word 'we' instead of 'I' throughout the negotiation.

Confidence and awareness!

It's important to feel good and to feel like yourself when you are in a challenging meeting. The value of power poses is often mooted by self-improvement experts (think of striking up that Superwoman pose in the bathroom), and there is no doubt that positive non-verbal communication can make a big difference to the impression you make on others.[33] Breathe! Smile! Be a great communicator. These actions will show your authority without you appearing bossy, and should also boost your confidence.

Silence is golden

It's so hard to manage the silences when you're nervous, especially in an interview/negotiation, but state what you want, then listen and wait for the other person to come back to you. If you fill that awkward space with self-deprecating lines such as, 'Of course, I totally understand if you can't', you make it easy for them to say no.

If you get shot down, don't give up

Even if the absolute worst happens, and your tough negotiation stance costs you a job offer/client, don't let that turn you into a scared little mouse when you go for the next one. Stating your worth will not injure you – it is what you deserve. No more, no less.

Overcome imposter syndrome and let go of perfectionism

Do you secretly feel like a fraud? Do you fear that your boss/colleagues/clients/everyone might discover the 'real' you and send you packing? Do you feel you're not working hard enough? Imposter syndrome and perfectionism may be holding you back.

Some 70% of women and men report experiencing impostor syndrome at some point in their lives.[34] The bad news is that it can actually knock your self-worth, make you feel dissatisfied and send your career into a decline, either by causing you to subconsciously sabotage yourself at work, or by overachieving to the point of burnout.

The good news is this doesn't have to be a permanent feature of your internal landscape. Here are a few tips to undo the negative thinking that goes with imposter syndrome:

- Recognize you have it and know that having it means you're not seeing things as they really are. This is the first step on the road to separating your paranoid imaginary version of yourself from the awesome you that others see.
- Celebrate your achievements! List the great stuff you've done at work recently. Expressing specific, positive thoughts about yourself will boost your confidence.
- Done is often better than perfect, so keep making decisions quickly and taking risks rather than striving for unachievable standards of perfection.
- Accept that no one feels confident and fabulous 100% of the time. That's life and that's OK. Confidence ebbs and flows.
- Don't forget, there will be a reason why you are prone to feeling like an impostor and it's probably not your fault. Maybe you were raised or educated in a super-competitive environment. Perhaps you work in an industry that tends to be judgemental. If things get really toxic, you might want to find some help and support and consider really taking charge of your life by exploring a new career avenue or a working arrangement where there's less of a cut-throat culture.

Think about the long term

Have clear goals for every year of your career and a plan for how you will get there. Invest in yourself and your skills. And, if things don't go as planned, don't get discouraged! If you don't fail, you don't learn.

Keep talking about money

We all need to get used to talking about money. The more often you practise money-talk on a daily basis, the more confident your conversational repertoire will become and the better every verbal financial transaction will be.

> ### REMEMBER, SALARY NEGOTIATION DOESN'T HAVE TO BE ALL ABOUT CASH
>
> **Sometimes you may have hit the upper pay limit and your employer won't be able to increase your salary band. Of course, getting paid at the level you want is key, but are there other things you could ask for too:**
>
> - *Pensions:* **Your employer has the obligation to put some money in your pension, but you can try to negotiate a higher contribution.**
> - *Benefits:* **Could you have health insurance? What does it cover?**
> - *Perks:* **These could be flexible working hours, shares, holidays or other perks such as training and personal development, financial wellness programmes, yoga classes, physio sessions, pets at work, unlimited holiday, etc.**
> - *Vacations:* **How many holiday days do you get?**
> - *Stock options:* **Having company shares or options (the right for you to buy shares in the future and at a certain price) means that you have an incentive to work hard and help the company grow, and entices you to stay with them for the long term. Remember that if you own shares in a business that is not listed you will have to wait (sometimes a long time) to sell your shares and will only make money if the sale is successful. I invite you to check the terms of these offerings as well as the tax treatments.[35]**

Earn More Money with a Side Project

Research by *Harvard Business Review* shows that when people spend just 15 minutes a day pursuing something they love and believe in, they report higher levels of well-being than those who don't.[36] So, even if you've decided to be practical and opt for a job that's a bit boring but well-paid for now, you don't have to give up doing what you love. Choose to devote some of your spare time to it, and it might even develop into a lucrative side project. Many start-ups began life like this.

You will often hear the term 'side hustle' but the reality is that it can often become overwhelming to manage both a full-time job and a side passion project you love – so make sure you practise self-care and don't glorify the hustle to avoid burnout.

Making a side project work

Whether you're saving up for something expensive or simply hoping to learn new skills and grow your professional network, running a side project can help.

Passion projects are paying out – Britons are earning £249 million from what was once thought of as mere hobbies.[37] A side project can also be a great source of income for saving up for a specific project or event. Anyone who has a special skill, from baking to design, may as well capitalize on it.

Some successful examples of side projects include:

- *renting out a spare room*
- *occasional blogging and podcast-making*
- *managing social media for small businesses*
- *selling your technical services, web design or copy editing on Fiverr or Upwork*
- *creating an online course with online platforms Udemy and Teachable*
- *selling old designer finds and furniture on eBay or Vinted*

Taking the Leap: Entrepreneurs and the Self-employed

Becoming an entrepreneur is certainly not for everyone, but it could be a great way to control your future and build an asset (i.e. your company) that generates income for you and your family for generations to come – and at the same time working on something you like.

Is entrepreneurship for you?

Can you deal with financial uncertainty or no salary for a while? Are you passionate about your mission and what you are building? Are you perseverant and resilient? If you answered yes to these questions, you might be ready to take the plunge and start building your start-up. What personally keeps me going building Vestpod is how passionate I am about empowering people financially, so working on something you're passionate about – whatever that may be – makes a huge difference!

It's usually a good idea to start with a side project while you're still employed to gauge your market and abilities. To transform a side project into a business, try your idea again and again in order to find a product market fit and understand if people would be ready to buy your products or services. (Ask yourself, too, could you keep running this as a side project rather than full-time?) If you'd like to understand the intensity and the work you'll be doing, you could also try getting a job in a start-up to get a taste for the entrepreneurial life.

Prepare yourself for some challenging times. It can take a long time for a business to take off, and many start-ups actually fail for a myriad of reasons, for example when they can't find a viable business model, run out of cash or have co-founder issues. For me, failing is not the end but it's how you learn.

Now ask yourself these final questions:

- *Do you love what you're doing so much that you're ready to take the plunge?*
- *What will your business look like? There are many types of business for different types of founders: you could be a freelancer, a 'company of one'*

(which is the title of an excellent book by Paul Jarvis) or actually build a team and make your first hires. Think about how much time you would want to spend working versus doing other things like spending time with your family – set boundaries if this is important for you.

- *Are you financially ready? By which I mean, do you have an emergency fund? Have you cleared all your bad debts? Also make sure as a founder that you pay yourself when and as soon as you can, because if you struggle financially that adds more risk to the business.*

If you're ready to take the plunge, you should try to launch the business on your own (bootstrapping it with your own money) or, if you know you will need funds to develop some technology for example, you will need to raise some money. Don't seek funding too early: today, the cost of launching a business online is very low and you can achieve a lot by building your website and leveraging existing platforms, writing code or content, or blogging and making videos, therefore building an audience. Prepare a business plan or run your numbers, and try to make your first sales. Then, once you have validated your assumptions and really need the money, start looking for the best investors. Choose carefully if you have the choice. This may take some time but can help you scale. Entrepreneurship is tough but you can do it!

Understanding your worth, working towards a good salary or rate that will help you to live comfortably and achieve your financial goals, and negotiating for more, are key to helping save more money. It is then in your hands to make sure you make the right spending and saving decisions and save for what you care about and for the future. But the valuable lesson is that money can come from many more places than just your regular pay packet. I hope this has got you thinking not only about your options in terms of side projects, freelancing and maybe building a business, but also your attitude towards valuing yourself and your services in the market.

* *

CHAPTER 5
NAVIGATING YOUR BANK BALANCE

* *

What you will learn in this chapter:
The difference between saving and investing money
Where to save money: savings accounts vs. ISAs
Where to invest money: pensions vs. ISAs vs. investment accounts

* *

We will begin this chapter by talking about the short term – how to save your money today. We will investigate the best ways to save money and what types of savings accounts/ISAs you can use. We will then move on to the long term and consider retirement planning and what pensions and stocks and shares ISAs can do for your money.

> **This chapter is UK-specific and is an explanation of the main financial products available to you. If you're not from the UK, you'll find tax-efficient equivalents for your money. If you don't understand a product, don't put money in it. I cannot tell you what's best for you, so do your research and talk to an adviser if necessary. Also check the latest rules on savings and tax allowances, this is not tax advice... Check the government website section 'Money and Tax'.[38]**

To Save or to Invest?

While we will deep dive into investing in the next chapter, we need to know the *difference* between saving and investing in order to be able to choose the right place to hold our money (current accounts, savings accounts, ISAs, pensions, etc.).

When you are *saving*, you have the foreknowledge that you will spend the money you are setting aside in the near future. You want this money to be safe and available anytime (it should be *liquid*), but you should ensure that you maximize the potential saving rate. This is why saving your spare cash in a savings account, although not very risky, is not letting your money work very hard for you. If you have some expensive debts, such as those on credit cards, pay off these first before saving if you can and check if there is a repayment cost. Check how much interest you are paying on your debts; if the cost is higher than what you receive or could receive on your savings, it may be a good idea to tackle these first (for example, a credit card not repaid in full can cost you around 18% in interest rates – a rate that will be impossible to get on savings). Also focus on building up your emergency savings to prevent you from ending up in debt again (see page 39).

Once you are comfortable you've built up your savings nest (including your emergency fund), don't touch it...you can start building another pot of savings that you could decide to use for investing. With *investing* you will be deploying your capital and putting your money to work. You want to make it grow by buying things that increase in value over time. When you invest money, it can be locked away for a certain period of time (i.e. if it is in property you would need to sell that real estate to receive the money; if it is in the stock market you would need to sell your investments). These investments are not as liquid as cash – and investing always involves some risk. Consider the risk carefully – you don't want to be forced into a position where you have to sell these investments quickly at a difficult time.

Short-term goals (1–5 years): You want your money to be available anytime, to keep your money in cash and save into cash deposits.

Medium-term goals (5–10 years): Again cash deposits might sometimes be the best answer. You could invest for certain goals.

Long-term goals (10+ years): You may want to consider investing. If you are willing to take more of a risk, you could make your money work harder. In Chapter 6 we will discuss in detail the concept of investing: inflation, compound interest and risk/reward.

EXERCISE

Based on the goals you identified in Chapter 2, can you decide for each of them if you would need to save or invest money?

Goal	Save or invest?	Description

Which Bank?

You may still have the bank account you chose ten years ago or you may have recently switched to something new, but you still need to assess if this is the right account for your money. There are a few guidelines that can help you choose the best account:

1. What comes as standard with the account? What is the cost?
2. What's your communication style?
3. How easy will it be to switch to this account?
4. What do the reviews (Trustpilot) say?

NEW BANKS VS. TRADITIONAL BANKS

Have you tried one of the new app-only banks? The likes of Monzo, Revolut and Starling Bank have tapped into a desire for seamless digital customer services and done away with bricks-and-mortar banking. The new banks focus all their energy on ease of use, offering a simple, multi-platform banking experience that makes the ins and outs of everyday personal banking just a click away.

Understanding what you need from a bank is crucial to your selection process: shop around, play the field and know what you want from them, and then make sure you choose the one that suits you:

- How much would you like to save?
- Will you be making regular contributions or a lump sum?
- Do you need instant access to your money?

With your newly formed requirements at your fingertips, you can now start to research various banks. Make sure you do this exercise over a few comparison sites because they may return different results or list different products, i.e. savings accounts or ISAs. Play with the different options and make sure you use the filters according to your bespoke banking needs. Once you have a selection of products you think could be suitable for you, do your own research and visit the provider's website.

Where to Save Your Money

Saving money is hard work but it can be hugely rewarding when it's done properly. There are three main things to look for when trying to decide where to save your money:

1. **Make sure you can access the money when you need it to achieve your goal:** Is that in two months? One year? Five years?
2. **Maximize the interest rate you are receiving on your savings:** In today's world, interest rates on savings are low, so it's challenging to find the best. (The rate used to compare savings accounts is called an Annual Equivalent Rate (AER) – the higher the better.) You can save in fixed or variable rate accounts; usually the longer you keep your savings with a provider, the higher the rate you get. But make sure the length of the rates is in line with the fixed period you envisage when you will need your money back.
3. **Ensure you save in a tax-efficient manner:** Do this unless the money is held in an ISA or the amount of interest you are getting falls below the Personal Savings Allowance (see below). This may not be relevant today in a low-rate environment, but it could be in the future if interest rates increase and you will be able to start making more money from your savings.

Be aware that the headline saving rate can be misleading; check the small print to understand how the interest rate is calculated.

TAXES ON INTEREST AND PERSONAL SAVINGS ALLOWANCE (PSA)

When you save money and receive interest on your savings, you have to pay tax on it! But these days most people can earn some interest from their savings without paying tax under the PSA.

For more information and the latest rules go to the government website section 'Tax-free Interest on Savings'.[39]

The main goal for you now is to save some money and make it grow in the form of interest. So, let's look at the best places for you to make your money work harder.

Current accounts

Your current account is where you do your day-to-day banking and transactions; it isn't usually a place in which to hold money for a long period of time, but recently some banks have started to offer higher interest rates on these accounts, so this is an option to consider. However, using your current account for savings could prove to be a dangerous option – should you look for a separate savings account in order to avoid spending all your money?

Savings accounts and premium bonds

- **'Instant' or Easy Access Savings Accounts:** If you know you will need to use the money very soon, then look out for the best saving rates across banks to get the most of your savings; the rates will be quite low because of the flexibility you are asking for.
- **Fixed Rate Savings Accounts:** You could save into a fixed-rate deposit (also called a fixed rate bond), which means that if you leave your money in the account for long enough (usually one to five years), you will receive interest that is higher than with normal savings accounts. You put money in at a given time and can take it out after the fixed term. If you want to take the money out earlier, you will have to pay a penalty.
- **'Regular' Saving Accounts/'Monthly Savers':** If you know you are a great saver and can commit to saving the same amount of money every month (say £20 or £200) for a fixed period of time, you can look into regular savings accounts.
- **Premium Bonds:** A premium bond is a savings product where the prize is decided by a lottery. Bonds are issued by National Savings and Investments (NS&I), a state-owned savings bank in the UK. They offer savers protection against principal loss and liquidity. There is a minimum and maximum amount you can hold and you don't earn any interest. This type of saving is flexible, as you can withdraw it at any time; you just lose the chance to win in the given month.

Choosing a savings account provider

I find it useful to allocate my savings to different goals and the easiest way to do this is to open one separate account for each goal (i.e. different pots of money). Allocating your savings is also super-motivating because you can label the accounts and see what you are saving for.

To get the best rates on your savings, you can start shopping around and use an online comparison website. They will show you the best on all the accounts but make sure you also do your own research. Depending on how hands-on you are likely to be bear in mind some accounts offer a high bonus rate which is designed to seduce you – but bonuses drop off after a certain period. Make sure you understand the terms.

ISAs (Individual Savings Accounts)

ISAs are savings accounts on which you never pay tax.[40] ISAs are tax-efficient, meaning that all the money sheltered in your ISA is protected from taxes for the long term: you won't be paying taxes on the interest earned, and the investments you hold in an ISA are protected from capital gains tax and income tax. For inheritance, you can pass on your ISA to your spouse/ civil partner without losing the tax advantage. The surviving partner is given an Additional Permitted Subscription (APS) allowance.

If you are living in the UK and are 16 or over, you get what is called an ISA allowance. You can put money into the four different types of ISA accounts that are available:

1. Cash ISA
2. Stocks and shares ISA
3. Lifetime ISA (cash or stocks and shares)
4. Innovative finance ISA

They have different specifications and we will look into these below. Some of them are used to save money and others to invest.

You can also choose whether you want to split your allowance between the different ISAs or put everything in one (just a quick note: there is a limit on the lifetime ISA!). Your allowances need to be utilized by 5 April each year, falling in line with the tax year, and cannot be carried forward. You will get a new allowance each year, but you won't be able to use the old one if you haven't used it fully. Each financial year you can open and contribute to only one of each type of ISA. Check the latest tax rules and allowance on the government website.[41]

You can move your ISA to another provider but never transfer an ISA yourself – always use the forms provided by the issuer. When switching from one provider to another, make sure you don't just withdraw the money and reopen an account somewhere else: the provider has to do this transfer for you so you don't lose the tax-free umbrella your ISA savings are under.

If you need to, you can withdraw your money from your ISAs but once it's out, you won't be able to pay it back in if you have reached your annual allowance limit. You will also lose the tax benefits on the money you have withdrawn.

If you are married, you can maximize your ISA allowances by utilizing your partner's allowance too if they do not use it.

For *saving* money, there are two ISAs you can choose from: cash ISA and cash lifetime ISA. Stocks and shares ISAs, stocks and shares lifetime ISAs and innovative ISAs are used for *investing* money (see Chapter 6).

Cash ISAs

With the cash ISA, shop around and look for the best interest rates: that's how you make money. As with saving accounts, you can compare and switch to the best provider. You can also choose from instant access, regular savers and fixed-rate ISAs. ISAs are important because you don't know what the future holds...the PSA could change and potentially go down as interest rates and saving rates go up. You could also be earning more and lose your PSA when you become a higher taxpayer. But that won't be the case with ISAs because anything that is saved or invested within an ISA will continue to earn interest tax-free as soon as it's under the ISA umbrella.

Lifetime ISAs

The lifetime ISA was launched to push savers to beef up their savings towards a deposit for a first home or for retirement. Think of it as a hybrid between a pension and an ISA.

To qualify you have to be between 18 and 40 (you can then contribute until you reach 50). There is no maximum monthly contribution, you save as little or as much as you want each month, up to a maximum yearly limit (the only minimum is the limit imposed by the ISA provider). Any savings you put into it before your 50th birthday will receive an added bonus from the government (see the government website for information on the current limits and bonus).[42]

You have two options for using the money in your lifetime ISA:

1. **Save for a first home:** Your savings and the bonus can be used towards a deposit on a first home (note that accounts are limited to one per person rather than one per home). So, two first-time buyers can each receive a bonus when buying together. The lifetime ISA cannot be used within the first 12 months of you opening the account.
2. **Save for retirement (after your 60th birthday):** You can take out all the savings tax-free at this stage. If you want to know if it's relevant for you to save for retirement into a lifetime ISA versus a pension, you should consult an adviser because it depends on your personal circumstances.

If you wanted to take the money out earlier for another reason you would have to pay a penalty on the value of the amount withdrawn.

It is worth noting that, with the lifetime ISA, both cash and stocks and share products are available, so if you decide you want to invest it (depending on your goals and when you need the money, and the risk you are willing to take), see Chapter 6.

HELP-TO-BUY ISAS

Help-to-Buy ISAs were available until 30 November 2019. If you already have one in place, you can keep saving into it until November 2029.[43]

For more information and details about conditions and allowances, etc. on savings accounts and ISAs, go to the government or MoneyHelper websites.[44]

Where to Invest Long-term and Retirement Savings

There is a high chance you are already saving for the long term and investing some money in your pension, especially if you are employed. If you're not, don't worry. To start investing you will first need to understand which accounts and structures are right for you.

When investing money, it's important to consider the tax implications and understand that there are a number of ways that you can invest in a **tax-efficient manner**. In the UK, the two most common tax-efficient investment vehicles are ISAs and pensions.

Again, get clued up on these products to understand what is best for you. You can consult an independent financial adviser for more help and always check the latest rules.

Pensions

Pensions are too often thought of as being just for older people, but the reality is that you should be contributing today towards your pension to make sure you have enough money to retire on. This long-term pocket isn't perhaps as exciting as your emergency fund or as urgent as paying off your expensive debts but it is just as critical to your quality of life. Luckily, pensions offer a *tax-efficient way* to invest in your retirement, and workplace pensions offer some sort of free money!

Looking at pensions, there are two main options: the state pension from the government and private pension schemes. You will see below that it's important to consider both.

State pension

The state pension is a weekly payment from the government that you can receive once you reach state pension age. Please note that, at the time of writing, the full state pension stands at £179.60 per week so is probably not enough to live on. In order to qualify for the state pension, you need to make NI contributions (NICs). To qualify for any pension at all you will need to have ten years of NICs. To qualify for the full new state pension, you will need to have 35 qualifying years, but this may increase with time.

If you are a parent who has stopped/decided to stop working and earning when you have children, don't forget to register to sign up for Child Benefit (even if you are not eligible, and for children under 12). Doing this will allow you to keep receiving NI credits that will be added to your NICs and, hopefully, allow you to make the most of your state pension when you retire.

Here's a shocker: if you're under 40, you probably won't receive your state pension until you're at least 70 years old (if not later). I don't know about you, but I don't really fancy working full-time at the grand old age of 70!

Not to be alarmist, but it's important you get to grips with state pensions today in order to plan ahead with confidence and also consider an additional private pension.

EXERCISE

You can check how much state pension you can get, and when and how to increase it, by creating an account and logging on to the government website.[45]

Why save into a pension at all?

When you earn money (above a certain level – the personal allowance, see page 63), you start paying tax. When you put money into a pension, instead of paying tax to the government on salary or income you receive, some will go directly into your pension – this is **tax relief**. This also works if you are saving into a pension and if you don't have any income (your partner, for example, can pay into your pension up to a certain amount). Essentially, the more tax you pay, the higher the tax relief.

Tax relief depends on your individual circumstances and could change in the future so always check the latest pension rules on the government's websites.[46]

When your pension is invested, your money can **grow largely free from tax**, so that means investments held within a pension (and also an ISA) grow faster than investments held outside these tax wrappers.

> # TAX RELIEF
>
> **For a basic rate taxpayer: If you have an employer they will deduct their pension contribution from your pay and send it to your pension provider who will add it to your account. The government will automatically top up the remaining amount.**
>
> **For the self-employed: You will make the contribution to your pension provider directly and the government will automatically put in the remaining amount.**
>
> **For a higher rate and top-rate taxpayer: You have to ask for the additional tax relief through your Self Assessment tax return.**

Private pension schemes

Fundamentally a private pension is a tax-free long-term savings plan that you, your employer (if you have one) and the government pay into. The money contributed to your pension over time is invested and will have the opportunity to grow until you retire.

The money is locked until you reach retirement age. Then when you want to start using the funds in your pension pot you can usually withdraw about 25% as a tax-free sum and use the remaining amount to pay yourself an income and/or irregular lump sums – which are taxable. Private pension schemes are workplace pensions and personal and stakeholder pensions.

Workplace pensions

All employers are required by law to offer a workplace pension scheme. This scheme is quite handy as it helps you save for retirement without doing all that much – and because workplace pensions are managed by pension providers, you don't need to be an ace at investing.

With **auto-enrolment**, you will be automatically enrolled to start saving a portion of each pay cheque (i.e. it is a 'salary sacrifice') – you only need to do something or take action if you choose not to save.

There are different types of pensions but it's likely that your money is in a **defined contribution (DC)** scheme. This means that contributions will be automatically deducted from your salary. Your employer will make contributions as well and you may be eligible to get tax relief from the government. If you can, pay as much as you can afford to (considering your other goals and personal circumstances) and don't leave money on the table. There is a minimum amount that has to be contributed by you, your employer and the government in the form of tax relief. But double-check because your employer could be offering a higher percentage contribution.

You are eligible if you work in the UK, are at least 22 years old and earn over a certain amount per year (check the government website for the latest guidance), and you will automatically be enrolled in the scheme.

You can opt out of the workplace pension if you like and rejoin later, and you can still start your own pension if you are a member of a workplace pension scheme.

Workplace pensions are quite a powerful way to save money, but it depends on your personal situation: for instance, if you feel as though you don't have enough to live on or are struggling to repay debt, think about whether you should prioritize your long-term future or immediate quality of life.

With a workplace pension, your employer has chosen a pension provider that will invest the money that you contribute. They manage your pension and the investments that go into your pension. You pay them a fee for this that will have been negotiated between your employer and the pension provider. You don't have to pay for it separately; it is charged directly as a percentage of the amount of money held in your pension. Make sure you look into your pension statements and understand how your pension is managed and invested. You or your pension provider will decide on particular investments based on the level of risk you choose and the time you have to retirement. You may want to check that you have an appropriate investment option and that you understand the **default option** your money is put into as it may not be adapted to your goals or is too conservative.

Use the workplace pension contribution calculator from the MoneyHelper website to find out, based on your age, gender and salary, what workplace pension contributions are made by you and your employer.[47]

EXERCISE

The **annual allowance** for pensions contributions is the maximum amount that can be contributed into a pension per annum (from you and your employer for example) – while still receiving tax relief. If you are a top-rate taxpayer, your annual allowance may be reduced for the tax year. This is called the tapered annual allowance. Don't hesitate to speak to an adviser about this.

If you are working super-hard towards putting money into your pension, bear in mind that there is a maximum you can pay into the pension and benefit from the tax relief. This is called the **lifetime allowance (LTA)**. This number is scheduled to increase every year based on inflation (consumer price inflation/CPI).

It may come as a surprise, but you probably won't get regular statements from your pension provider, so it's worth checking with them how much you have in your pension and what the performance has been over recent years.

Personal and stakeholder pensions

These are private pensions that you pay directly into. You pick a pension provider and start contributing on your own; your pension provider will claim tax relief at the basic rate and add it to your pension pot if you are a basic rate taxpayer, otherwise you will need to fill in a Self Assessment tax return to get the extra tax relief.

A personal pension is a popular choice among self-employed people and can also be used if you are not working. The drawback of being self-employed is that it's entirely up to you to make sure you're on track with your savings and pension, and you don't receive an employer contribution.

One type of personal pension that has proven to be very popular is the self-invested personal pension (SIPP). A SIPP is a DIY pension where you can choose what your money is invested in and you have full control of your pension pot. You can choose to build your own balanced portfolio with your own risk profile. You are also free to choose some more specific investments that may not be available through a workplace pension.

This can be a big responsibility for you, so you either have to swot up or get help from an adviser. If you already have a workplace pension but would like more flexibility managing your money, you could open a SIPP as well.

One of the great tax advantages of a SIPP is that it allows you to pass on your pension to your beneficiaries on your death. Your beneficiaries can normally choose to take the pension fund as a lump sum or leave it invested in a SIPP.

There is another type of personal pension called a stakeholder pension. These pensions have specific government requirements, for example limits on charges.

How to manage an existing pension

Many people can easily lose track of how many old workplace pension pots they have. You can use the pension-tracing service to track down a lost pension and check your pension statements to see how much you have and how it's invested.[48]

EXERCISE

- If you already have a pension in place: do you know how it is invested, how it has been performing and what level of fees you are paying? Do you know the level of risk on your investments? It may be a good idea to ask HR who your pension adviser is and set up a meeting with them to find out.

- Based on the retirement calculator you used for Chapter 3, are you happy with your level of contributions or could you save more?

Should you consolidate your pensions?

If you discover that you have some old pensions, you can potentially transfer them and put them all into one pot. You will need to decide if that makes sense for you; it could make your life easier to see all your retirement money in one place and may also reduce the fees you would have been paying on individual pots. But at the same time, there is a risk that you could lose pension benefits and get charged fees. It's always best to discuss consolidation with a financial adviser beforehand. After you've made your decision, either the adviser can help you to consolidate or you can do this transfer yourself by contacting your pension provider. You can also use an app to consolidate your pensions.

Pensions are complex and, in order to make sure you have enough saved to live well in retirement, do seek independent financial advice.

Stocks and shares ISAs/stocks and shares lifetime ISAs

The difference between the previously discussed cash ISA and the stocks and shares ISA is that the latter is invested in the stock market. With the cash ISA, you save so your money is available at any time; with the stocks and shares ISA, you want to invest to make your money work in the long term. Which is also much more risky (*the value of your investments can go up and down*), and that's why you expect a higher return! When you want to take money out of a stocks and shares ISA, there is an additional step of selling the investments (stocks and funds) held within this ISA: you can't predict the future value (you don't want to be under pressure to do this in case the markets are not performing well). A stocks and shares ISA is more flexible than a pension; you don't have to wait to retire to access your money.

The way this type of ISA works is that you invest your money in the stock market where all income, capital gains and interest are tax-free.

Head over to Chapter 6 for a detailed explanation of investing on the stock market and choosing your stocks and shares ISA and stocks and shares lifetime ISA.

The Innovative Finance ISA

The Innovative Finance ISA allows you to invest in Peer-to-Peer (P2P) loans rather than cash or shares. You can lend money via the main P2P platforms to small businesses or individuals and expect them to pay you some interest until you hopefully get your money back. The risk is much higher than with cash savings so understand what you invest in. The ISA tax wrapper means the interest you receive on the loans are not subject to tax.

General investment accounts

A general investment account (or brokerage account) is one where you can buy, hold and sell investments. With a general account, any dividends you receive from your shares or any capital gain will be taxed above the allowance, unlike with your ISA or pension.

Investments (in stocks and shares ISAs or held within an investment account) are also covered by the FSCS in case the institution holding your investments has gone into default. Ensure that this is the case with your current provider.

You may or may not need some or all of the accounts and products presented in this chapter, but it should give you an overview of what's on offer and the financial products you may have heard of over the years. As life becomes more complicated you may be using more of these accounts to fund yourself. If there are chunks of text that don't yet apply to you, save them for when they do; what you need to ensure is that you take responsibility for your own money education. *Small changes make a big difference over time.*

CHAPTER 6
INVESTING
FOR THE
LONG TERM

* *

What you will learn in this chapter:

The rewards and risks of investing

How financial markets work

How to build a balanced portfolio

* *

Investing is key to building financial security. With investing, you want your money to work harder for you, outpace inflation (the price of goods and services are going up every year) and benefit from compound growth. In this chapter, we will talk about misconceptions, how investing works and how you can get started. While it's important to have cash savings, playing it safe by stashing all your money away in low-interest savings accounts is actually risky too because your money will lose value over time. So, consider saving for the short to medium term and invest for the long term!

How can investing make your money work harder?

Economically, when we think about investing, we are purchasing something today that we hold on to because we anticipate using it in the future to add to our wealth. For example, you can invest in education, financial markets or property.

In finance, investments are something you buy or put your money into with the aim of getting a profitable return or income. There are many types of investments that you can make, and they all have very different characteristics and will offer different risk and return. These investments are called 'assets'.

Assets are the things you own. An 'asset class' is a group of investments with similar risk/return characteristics. There are four main asset classes:

1. **Cash:** It's supposedly the least risky because if cash is held in a bank it's almost impossible to lose it. At the same time, the interest you receive is usually lower than that for other asset classes because of this lower risk level.
2. **Bonds:** When buying a bond, you loan some money to a company in exchange for a fixed interest payment called a 'coupon'.
3. **Stocks and shares:** When you buy a share you buy a (small) part of a company in exchange for potential dividends and expect an increase in share price.
4. **Property:** Buying a home or investing in real estate.

So how do these investments help you to grow your money?

1. **You make a profit/loss when you sell them:** You buy an asset (such as a share or a house) and it increases/decreases in value. In the future, you will sell that same asset for a better price, therefore you make a gain – if it's for less you make a loss. This is also called 'capital gain', i.e. you make a gain/loss on the capital you invested.
2. **You earn an income:** You buy an asset and it's going to provide you with some future income (i.e. you make regular money from it, such as buying a house and renting it out or receiving dividends from shares).

These benefits are called a *'return'* on your investment: returns are the profits or losses you get from your investments.

'ALTERNATIVE' INVESTMENTS

There are also many other 'alternative' investments available that you may have heard of (that we will not be covering here), such as cryptocurrencies, stakes in start-ups, foreign currency (FX), 'collectibles' (such as wine, art, jewellery or antiques), private equity, commodities, and many, many more. These types of investments are traded (i.e. bought and sold) outside of traditional stocks and bonds markets. They often require a special interest or expertise and have been mostly the domain of wealthy investors looking for diversification and a potential for higher returns – meaning higher risk-taking than with more traditional investments. We now see more and more retail investors looking at these alternative investments, so if you've been learning about some of these, make sure you clearly understand the risks associated with them – for example: not liquid (it can be hard and take years to sell your stake in a private business and you may not see your money back), volatile (cryptocurrencies), requires very specific knowledge and skills (art), etc. – and that these only constitute a small part of your overall investments. If you don't understand it, don't invest in it!

Are You Ready to Invest?:
Your Pre-investment Checklist

First off, to boost the chances of your investing journey going smoothly (i.e. you making the highest return for the level of risk you are ready to accept), you need to be able to have money available to invest in the **long run** – anywhere between five to ten years (ideally ten years+). Which means not seeing that cash again for quite a long time. So, if you're looking to have immediate access to your funds for an emergency, investing is not what you need. As previously discussed, I would recommend having at least three to six months' living expenses squirrelled away in a cash savings account **(emergency fund) and repaying any expensive debts** (such as credit cards) before you begin to invest.

Next, you need to accept that investing involves a level of **risk**. Nobody likes to lose their hard-earned money, but if you're depending on that investment to make a guaranteed return and can't afford to lose a penny, proceed with caution, as there are no guarantees that this will definitely accumulate, and you may not get back what you invested. Financial markets (the 'market') are unpredictable and they wax and wane constantly.

Finally, when deciding to invest money, it's important to remind yourself of your **goals**. Are you saving for retirement 30 years away, a home or further education? Once you have it clear in your own mind, you'll find it easier to make the right decisions about when to start moving your money, and when to leave it alone; and when to invest vs. when to save. Different goals have different time horizons and therefore different risk levels.

The best way to shake off the fear of investing is to educate yourself and start small. You don't have to be an expert before you start investing, but **if you don't understand it, don't invest in it**. Financial institutions make investment sound complicated and, sure, some aspects of it can be, but the basis of investing is pretty straightforward. If you lack confidence about investing and would like someone to help you out, make sure you contact a financial adviser.

You can always make excuses for not investing because it seems complex, it's laden with jargon and, if you are a woman, it's traditionally viewed as a 'man's thing' to do... Whatever your excuse, you need to shift your thinking now: it's time to change your preconceptions and negative concerns, and reframe your narrative. Think of investment as a smart, necessary strategy for making your money work for you. Once you see it that way, you'll feel empowered to take action.

Why Invest for the Long Term?

People invest their money for many different reasons. Investing is extremely personal and my reasons for investing money will probably be completely different from yours.

Grow your money and achieve your goals faster

Investing is an opportunity to build your wealth and achieve financial independence. The money you save and invest today will be used by your future self, so make sure you start saving early.

With pensions, you benefit from tax relief and, potentially, employers' contributions – all of which adds to your retirement pot. When interest rates are low, you could benefit from higher returns with investing than keeping your money in cash or in a savings account. Investing money also means it's locked away, so there's no chance of you spending it!

Investing can help you make your money work harder (with the help of compound interest) than just saving it in an ordinary bank account.

What is 'compound interest'?
The beauty of compound interest is that interest builds on interest, making a cash deposit or an investment grow at a faster rate than simple interest. Another way to see it is that the money you generate is reinvested to earn more money. The longer you can let your money grow and compound, the more money you will have in the end.

Here is a simple calculation to show how compound interest works:

You save £100 today in a cash deposit at a saving rate of 2%; at the end of the year you receive £2 in interest so finish the year with £102. Next year you will receive interest on £102 (not £100 anymore because you are leaving your money invested, right?), i.e. £102 x 2% = £2.04, so you end the year with £104.04. And so on, and so on... After five years, you have £110.41.

With compound interest, your money grows over time.

On a larger scale, say a £1,000 investment, this is how it works whether you save or invest (at different annual interest rates):

Annual interest rate

		1%	2%	5%	10%	15%
Years	1	£1,010	£1,020	£1,050	£1,100	£1,150
	5	£1,051	£1,104	£1,276	£1,611	£2,011
	10	£1,105	£1,219	£1,629	£2,594	£4,046
	15	£1,161	£1,346	**£2,079**	£4,177	£8,137
	20	£1,220	£1,486	£2,653	£6,727	£16,367
	25	£1,282	£1,641	£3,386	£10,835	£32,919

To understand how compound interest can work for you, you can use an Excel spreadsheet or an online compound interest calculator.

What is inflation?

Money today is worth more than money tomorrow. But money today does not buy as much stuff as five, ten or twenty years ago. And this phenomenon is known as *inflation*. Inflation measures the rate of increase in the price of goods and services in a country's economy. The ONS collects monthly prices for a basket of 700 everyday goods (so in total 180,000 prices). These prices then determine the Consumer Prices Index (CPI). This is the inflation measure used in the government's inflation target (but there are other measures of inflation).

You can buy something that costs £100 today. Now imagine inflation is kicking in at 2% per annum; in one year's time the price of this same item will be £102. But you still have your £100 since the money you have is in cash. That means you would become poorer by £2 and you now can't afford to buy this item anymore. In this example £2 is not a lot, but imagine ten years from now, with a constant inflation rate of 2% (but this can be a lot more!) – this item will cost £122, and so now you will be £22 worse off. You can check the current inflation on the ONS website.[49]

When you invest money you are looking to at least maintain your purchasing power. So, putting all your money into a cash savings account may not always be a good idea. In fact, experts have even coined a name for this strategy – 'reckless caution'. Inflation could eat away at your purchasing power; making your cash savings worth less and less over time.

INTEREST RATES

The Monetary Policy Committee (MPC) is a committee of the Bank of England (BoE) that votes on what the 'base rate' of interest should be in order to deliver monetary and financial stability for the people of the UK.

An interest rate is what you earn on your money when you save it with a bank, and it's also the cost of borrowing money. It's a percentage of the total amount borrowed.

The base rate helps manage inflation better. Changes in the base rate will impact both your savings and loans. A higher interest rate should (in theory) mean that you earn more interest (cash) on your savings and equally it should mean that you pay more interest on your loans. But it's a bit more complicated since providers are not obliged to reflect the change in interest rates since their internal rates also take into account current market conditions.

If you want to read more, check out the informative BoE website.[50]

Demystifying Investing

I want to demystify investing for you so that you find the confidence to learn more and get started with your own investments if you think it is for you. We'll start by unpicking those common myths that may be holding you back.

Myth 1: Investing = gambling

Fundamentally, gambling usually has an immediate and binary outcome, e.g. 'red' you win or 'black' you lose. If you invest in a single stock and the value of this stock goes to zero, then you also lose all your money. But with investing you can diversify your investments by putting money across a lot of shares, bonds and/or funds so that if one does fall in value, it will only have a small impact on your portfolio. This way, it is then unlikely you will lose all your money.

With investing, the outcome is rarely judged on a very short-term basis and the value of your investments can fluctuate. Which means that if the value of the market declines as soon as you have invested, you are not forced to lock in those losses but instead you have the luxury of waiting for the market to rebound – as it usually does over the long term.

Myth 2: I have to be rich to invest

Not anymore – there are a lot of online platforms that allow you to start small and invest regularly. As long as you follow the golden rule of not investing more than you can afford, you can make even the smallest sums work harder. Set up an automatic transfer with one of the handy apps and squirrel away those little nuggets in a place where, unlike a current account, they will eventually grow into a fund that is bigger in the long term.

Myth 3: I need someone to invest my money for me

Investing is now very accessible and, depending on how much support you need from your investment platform, you can manage your own portfolio. Robo-advisers will do this for you (see page 112), while you'll have more flexibility with self-investment platforms (see page 113). Of course, you might want to undergo a session with a financial adviser if you don't feel confident enough to get started. Setting up an investment account is relatively easy and there are lots of 'basic' options that offer low-cost and diversified exposure to the financial markets.

Myth 4: It's really expensive to invest money

Investing does always cost money, as does working with an adviser. However, opportunities for investing are now widely available and there are many options for the newbie investor at a range of prices. Online platforms and investing money into low-cost funds (a pool of money from a lot of investors) can help you keep your expenses low, which means – depending on your performance – more money in the future.

The Risks of Investing and How to Mitigate Them

There is obviously risk associated with investing in financial markets because the future is uncertain and most economic, business, political or other factors and events can cause uncertainty and have an impact on the market. It's inevitable that the market will go up and down, but there are ways to mitigate risks:

- **Time** is one of the key components of investing – investing means thinking **long term**. There's no point investing in the financial markets for a year then taking your money out. This is a long game. Markets are quick to react to events and are volatile; their prices go up and down. So, if you are investing for the short term (one to five years), you expose your money to ups and downs in value. If you wait longer, you have more chances for your investments to recover from these shocks.

- **Rises and falls** are painful, but they're part of life on the stock market. An investor must be prepared for them. But, of course, past performance isn't a guide to the future. With the 'stock market', experts often say, '**time in the market beats timing the market**', meaning that actually being invested in the market is better than trying to find the best time to invest.
- **Investing smaller amounts** regularly is often considered less risky than investing all your money in one go. When you **drip feed** into the market, you invest when the market is sometimes high, sometimes low. No one can predict market performance (also called '**pound cost averaging**'), but investing regularly can help smooth out your returns and ride out market bumps. When you invest a lump sum immediately, you are 'in the market' sooner rather than later because of the power of compound interest and the positive effect of time but, at the same time, you may end up buying when markets are high and don't know what tomorrow will bring…
- **Diversification** is also a way of reducing potential risks and improving returns when spreading your money across different types of investments or asset classes – not putting all your eggs in the same basket to avoid breaking them all.

It makes sense to be able to take more risk while you are young, because when you invest money, time is playing in your favour because of your capacity to absorb loss (i.e. recover lost savings with future income, which a retiree doesn't have the ability to do) and take less risk when your time horizon is shorter, when you approach retirement for example. But in the end, what matters most is how you personally feel about taking risk. *Are you comfortable with the fact that you may lose money? Can you handle very volatile markets? Or would you prefer something more stable? The higher the potential return, the more risk you usually have to accept.* The level of risk you will be willing to take will be represented by your investment portfolio and your asset allocation, and this is a very personal decision!

But you also need to **reframe risk** and think about the cost of not investing now: not investing your money can also make you 'lose' money over time, as you have less and less purchasing power and your money is not benefiting from compound growth.

How Does the 'Market' Work?

When a company needs money to grow (e.g. to finance an acquisition or new development), they can raise money on the stock market through an initial public offering (IPO) whereby they sell some of their stock, but they can also issue bonds.

What are shares?

When you invest in shares, you are buying a stake in a company and become a shareholder in that company – also called having equity in a company. Investing in shares is popular because historically the returns have been superior to those generated by cash and bonds. But at the same time, investing in shares is much riskier.

The terms 'stocks' and 'shares' can be used interchangeably, but 'stock' is a general term used to describe the ownership certificates of any company, and 'shares' refers to the ownership certificates of a particular company.

Shares derive their **value** from future profits and, therefore, today's price is based largely on investors' perceptions of what the company's future profits will be. If people think the company will do well and is undervalued at the moment, they will start buying company shares and the share price will go up, then investors may think they become 'overvalued' and so sell them.

Companies can also remunerate their shareholders in the form of **dividends**, i.e. part of the company's profits each year. You will probably get dividends from more established companies that are generating profit, but you might not get rapid growth. Dividends represent an income for you.

What are bonds?

When you invest in bonds, you are lending money to a company (i.e. corporate bonds) or to a government (i.e. gilts in the UK) for a fixed period of time. This asset class is also called 'fixed income'. In exchange for this investment the companies or governments will pay you interest, called a 'coupon', and at the end of the fixed period, you will receive your initial investment back. Investing in bonds is usually considered more risky than holding cash but less risky than investing in shares.

Gilts or government bonds are usually safer than corporate bonds if they are offered by 'safe' governments. Gilts offered by the UK government will be considered low risk because there is a low chance the UK will default on its bonds (i.e. not repay your nominal investment and interest rates) but at the same time, when the risk is lower the returns are lower!

Your investment in bonds can also be affected by inflation if the interest you receive is lower than the inflation rate (although some inflation-linked bonds or 'linkers' do exist and pay you an inflation-beating return). There is also a risk linked to the companies not being able to repay you the money you lent them; they may possibly default on the payment. This is why if you are considering bonds in your portfolio make sure they are investment grade, i.e. of good quality. Bonds are given 'ratings' that represent the likelihood of the debt being repaid, and are published by credit rating agencies such as Moody's, Standard & Poor's and Fitch. You may also have heard of the risky 'junk bonds': a high-yield or non-investment-grade bond, carrying a low rating – which means a higher default rate!

Bonds offer investors a way to diversify their portfolios away from shares because of their stable and relatively lower volatility. Also, bondholders have higher seniority than stockholders in the event that a company declares itself bankrupt.

What is a portfolio?

Once we get the concept of how shares and bonds work we can start thinking about putting them together in a portfolio, or a basket of investments.

In order to diversify (you don't want to buy just one share in one company), you want to build a portfolio of shares and bonds that is 'balanced', meaning it contains shares and/or bonds in a proportion that you work out. What you are trying to do with your portfolio is to limit the risk and to increase your return. Shares and bonds have a different risk–reward profile so having both in your portfolio can help you manage risk better.

Building a Diversified Investment Portfolio

Should you invest in individual shares or funds?

Shares and bonds are asset classes and you can invest in them directly ('*direct investing*'). Funds offer more diversification by bundling many stocks and bonds into one investment (potentially hundreds!). A fund is a portfolio of investments; they are not assets per se, they are a method of investing in traditional asset classes such as shares, bonds, commodities, property, etc. There are many stocks and/or bonds in a fund and prices for some of these can go down, but because you have a diverse portfolio, some other prices may go up at the same time, and as a result don't impact the performance of your portfolio as much as if you had just a few stocks and/or bonds. That helps spread your risk.

You may think that you can also try to achieve **diversification** yourself by investing in a lot of shares and bonds, but there is a decent chance that the trading costs of owning lots of stocks would be quite expensive (and materially hurt your returns) and/or that you wouldn't have the time/discipline to actively manage such a large portfolio.

Many investors with a more **passive approach** to investing (i.e. you're not a trader and don't have time to fully research the companies, want to leave your money to grow and don't move it around every day) tend to build portfolios with funds. Once you're happy with your portfolio and are excited about the prospect of doing more, you could consider allocating a portion of your investments to individual stocks e.g. 5–10%.

YOU'RE NOT A TRADER

Investing has come to be quite the trendy buzzword. Yet, because we often lack the necessary education and knowledge when it comes to investing, some of us think that investing equals simply picking a few stocks at a low price and selling them off at a higher price to make a quick buck.

But please, don't follow the hype! Instead of following your friends' investment 'advice', do your own research. You need to have a base-level understanding of what it is you're investing in, and you definitely should only invest as much as you could afford to lose.

Buying and selling investments and hoping to profit from small price fluctuations is something I don't recommend. In fact, I honestly think it's one of the more sure-fire ways to lose money. Day traders need to monitor the markets constantly. Not only is it exhausting, but it's also just not a good idea overall. You have to understand the market forces that impact pricing, which in and of itself is no easy feat.

What is passive investing?

Passive investing is an investing strategy that tracks, i.e. mimics, the performance of the market (a **benchmark** – a measure used to analyse the risk/return of a portfolio in order to understand how it is performing).

Passive investing is the opposite of **active investing**: when a professional is managing investments and trying to beat the market (benchmark), those investments are actively managed. The fund manager who actively tracks every bubble, wobble and weird echo in the market on your behalf will also usually take a fee.

The merits of 'active' vs. 'passive' have been debated for a while. So you might want to read more on the subject and work out which one is best for you.

What are the different types of funds?

Unit trust/OEIC: This is a pool of money invested in shares and/or bonds and passively or actively managed – this is what investors usually call a 'fund'.

Investment trusts: These are listed companies with shares that trade on the stock market. They invest in shares and/or bonds of other companies with the money they raise. They then divide the trust portfolio into units that you could buy or sell.

Index fund (also called an index tracker): This is a type of fund or Exchange Traded Fund (ETF) that is tracking the performance of a stock market index – a series of numbers that shows changes in the average prices of shares on a particular stock market over time. For example, the Financial Times Stock Exchange 100 Index (also called the FTSE 100 Index, FTSE 100, FTSE or, informally, the 'Footsie') is a share index of the 100 companies listed on the London Stock Exchange with the highest market capitalization. By investing in the fund, the investor gets diversification because they are not exposed to one stock but to all 100 stocks in the index. Index funds are passive; they 'just' replicate the performance of the market but are not trying to beat it!

So, if your market of choice is the FTSE All Share, you would effectively have a small share in every single company listed on it. When the market goes up, so does your money, and vice versa. If one day a new company is added to the market, the algorithm that controls your fund would add that into your group of stocks. If one leaves, it automatically drops off your list.

ETF (Exchange Traded Fund): This is a fund that is similar to unit trusts or OEICs but the difference is that ETFs are traded on a stock exchange, just like company shares. They can be actively or passively managed. Sometimes ETFs are more difficult for small investors versus unit trusts: with unit trusts, you can buy a fraction of a share – allowing small investors to invest and rebalance easily. ETFs are not divisible, except via a robo-adviser (or other model portfolio service: a selection of portfolios that you/an adviser can choose from to suit your risk profiles and investment objectives), which makes it harder for small investors to buy the appropriate amount and rebalance their portfolio. (See page 118 to learn about rebalancing.)

How to decide your asset allocation

When you want to start building your portfolio, you have to find the balance of shares and bonds in your portfolio – i.e. of funds – appropriate to the level of risk and reward you are seeking to achieve your goals.

- **'Stock funds' (or equity funds):** Your money is pooled with that of other investors and primarily invested in stocks of numerous publicly listed companies as an investment strategy.
- **'Bond funds':** Your money is pooled with that of other investors and primarily invested in bonds.
- **'Balanced funds':** Your money is pooled with that of other investors and primarily invested in a mixture of stocks and bonds.

The more time you have available, the more risk you can usually afford to take on. You want to gradually reduce your risk as you grow older, because when you retire you don't have the luxury to wait for the market to recover.

If you have a lot of time to achieve your goal(s) and you want to be exposed to more risk, you can usually take a higher proportion of shares vs. bonds in your portfolio. If you don't have that much time, want to reduce your risk and are OK with lower returns, you can take a higher portion of bonds in your portfolio.

This decision is personal and has to be your own investment strategy. Ask yourself:

Are you investing to protect your capital, to gain additional income or grow your wealth?

How much risk are you willing to take?

How long are you investing your money?

What kind of returns are you expecting?

Do you want to manage your investments or work with an adviser?

How often will you be checking your investments and making changes?

How much will it cost you?

There is a rule of thumb in personal investing for retirement savings, the *100 Minus Age Rule*: take 100 and subtract your current age (100 – 30 years old = 70). The result in percentage is how much of your portfolio could be invested in stocks. The remainder would be invested in bonds. According to Investopedia, this rule is now outdated: we live longer so we have to save more money and have more time for our money to grow.[51] At the same time, bonds are not paying as much as they used to, so investors may want to be exposed to a higher proportion of shares. The 'investment pros' have updated the rule to the '110 Minus Age' or even '120 Minus Age' for the greater risk-takers.

This is a basic guideline for retirement savings and really just a starting point for your journey into the world of investing. You should really be handling the risk you are personally comfortable with, taking into consideration your age, circumstances (women live longer than men) and whether you can you afford to lose this money.

Based on this rule, you can adjust the proportions for shorter time horizons for each of your goals: if you need the money earlier, you could adjust the proportions for fewer shares and more bonds. If you want to get ideas of asset allocation you can use online platforms offering risk questionnaires, which show you examples of asset allocation you could use.

Based on your financial plan, you can decide to work on one goal at a time, or a few different goals and prioritize them. Remember, focus on repaying expensive debts and building your emergency savings first, and then look at your other goals. You should review these regularly to see where to allocate your money and potential investments.

Set Your Mission for Investing

Before beginning to invest, you need to set out your investment philosophy – a set of guiding principles that inform and shape your investment decision-making process. And because investing is very personal (we all have different objectives, different appetites for risk and different personal circumstances), it's important to spend some time thinking about why you are investing. Your investment philosophy should contain the following:

- Learning about how the markets work: How investors behave and why markets fluctuate.
- Defining your attitude to risk on a goal-by-goal basis: No need to be consistent for all goals. You may not want to take the same risk for all.
- Research: Spend time researching what you can invest in and where (industries, sectors, megatrends, etc.). Do you expect growth or return over the coming years?
- Setting your values: Are you a social investor? What are your interests?

Remember: Markets may come and go but your investment philosophy should remain the same!

Do you know why you are investing and what you want to achieve? Make sure you revisit your goals and the time horizon regularly as your personal situation may change over time.

How to Start Investing

Working with an adviser or a wealth manager

If your situation is complicated or if this is all jargon and seems too overwhelming, you can always talk to a financial adviser and/or wealth manager. They will be able to assess your goals and risk, and recommend what could work well for you. They can then make your investments for you, but of course this comes at a price because you will have to pay for their advice on top of what you pay for the actual investment fees, usually as an ongoing percentage of the value of your investments.

If you have a workplace pension, perhaps this would be a good place to start, as you already have an account in place with some investments in the stock market (see page 87).

The DIY approach

If you have reached this point, congratulations! I know how it feels to buy your first investment. It's a long process. You may not have mastered all the investment concepts yet but you feel it's the right time to start.

Before starting to pick your funds, you need to open an account with an investment platform. A platform is an online service that allows you to select, buy and sell funds and stocks, and also monitor the market and receive market updates. At first it can be overwhelming to choose which one would be right for you.

It all depends on how much experience you have with investing, how DIY you want to be, your investment goals, what your tax-efficient options are (pension, ISA) and the level of fees you are willing to pay. Remember that the more help you get, the more fees and charges you usually pay.

Further, choosing an investment platform is not set in stone; you may want to start with something more hands-on and, once you've learnt the tricks of the trade, move to something more autonomous which you feel you have more control over. The market has evolved a lot in recent years and the arrival of the newish robo-advisers provides a solution for complete beginners to start investing.

There are two main categories of investment platforms out there, depending on how hands-on you want to be with your investments:

Robo-advisers: These are automated online investment services trying to bring investing to the masses. They offer investors ready-made bundles of investments. Great for the newbie investor, robo-advisers select your investments, rebalance and trade on your behalf. Visit vestpod.com for some of the better-known UK robo-advisors.

To use a robo-adviser, the usual method is to take an online questionnaire that will assess your investment goals, financial history, attitude to risk and finances at a point in time, and risk-profile you. From this, an algorithm makes a portfolio suggestion.

This portfolio is usually composed of low-cost, passive investments that track certain indices, including ETFs. Although called 'robo-advisers', these platforms don't all offer advice, but some do! As an investor, you don't have much to do – buying, selling and rebalancing is done for you by the robo. You receive information and market updates.

Robo pros	Robo cons
• Robos are fully automated. This means there's no face-to-face interaction with an adviser and enrolment is also automated	• Robos don't actually personally know you like an adviser would! There are no emotional ties or considerations. For example, it won't know that you're trying to change jobs, or you're thinking of starting a family or buying a house
• Your portfolio will be selected for you based on your goals and risk	• When investing, make sure you understand the market and its various fluctuations – but, most of all, how they'll affect you. A robo-adviser unfortunately won't call you to tell you of these changes!
• There is a chance that the robo will do the diversification better than you would! They will invest in a mix of funds (sometimes up to 20) that you may find it hard to achieve, plus they diversify globally	• They haven't all been on the market for a long time so the track record for some is not yet available
• Robos rebalance your investments for you	• They are pretty inflexible: you have to leave your money invested the way they decide and cannot add your own investments or modify the portfolio on offer
• It's an easy way to start investing – plus you'll be exposed to different markets very quickly	
• Set-up is quick and easy	
• Platforms are user-friendly and usually offer an app	

Self-investment platforms: These are online platforms that allow you to buy and hold a range of funds (and shares) and build your own portfolio. They will also provide you with some research and information on the funds, as well as their performance, but ultimately you will be in charge of making your own financial decisions. These platforms are 'execution-only' – which means that they will put your money into the investments you choose, not into what they tell you to buy. Some high-street banks may also provide this type of service.

In addition, lots of platforms may offer a premium service (**model portfolio service**): they will offer you some help to get you started and can provide an example portfolio or help you build your first portfolio based on your risk profile and investment objectives. Visit vestpod.com for some of the better-known UK self-investment platforms.

Self-investment pros	Self-investment cons
• You can choose your investments and build your portfolio yourself, which is great for experienced investors: it gives you freedom	• You can choose your investments and build your portfolio yourself, which is not always suitable for newbie investors
• Premium service is an easy way to get started	
• Easy to access	

How to choose an investment platform

Once you've decided the level of support you need from your platform based on your goals and level of involvement, you can start comparing them:

- Accounts on offer: Can you open a pension and the type of ISA you're looking for?
- Minimum investment and size of portfolio: What is the minimum investment required by the investment platform? Some platforms just ask for a lump sum to be invested while others may ask for regular contributions to your account.
- Range of investments: Not all platforms offer all investments. Would you like to hold funds and ETFs as well as shares? Do you want to be able to choose your funds (some platforms don't offer all the funds on the market)? If you use a robo-adviser to invest your money, you will not be able to choose the funds or stocks in your portfolio – the robo-adviser will do this for you.
- Ease of use: Investing can be overwhelming, so how easy is it to open an account? How easy it is to navigate their page? Can you ask questions?

- Data and research: Some platforms may be more suited to beginners than others and you can decide on the ones you prefer by visiting their websites and assessing the level of research, analysis and education they provide.
- Customer service: Do you want to deal with real humans or with an integrated chatbot? Are they quick replying to your requests?
- Charges and fees: Sometimes platforms have ongoing charges/annual fees (a fixed percentage of your investments or a fixed fee per month or year); sometimes it's a fixed fee per trade (dealing fees). This is why it's also important to decide how often you will be trading and get the most value for your money from your platform.
- Protection: You have some protection when the platform you're investing with goes under. Under the FSCS, you will qualify for FSCS protection worth up to a certain amount (see page 28). Always check your platform is regulated by the FCA and protected by the FSCS.

Check the ratings and consumer comments on Trustpilot. Use comparison websites to make sure you choose the right platform for your needs and, remember, this is not a definitive choice – you're not married to a platform, you're the client, and you can always transfer your money elsewhere.

How much money do you need to get started?

You don't need a lot of money to start investing and actually it's better to start small. The key for me is to get some 'skin in the game', which means that when you have incurred risk (monetary or otherwise) by being involved in achieving a goal (putting money in the stock market and taking some risk) you will learn a huge amount. You should experience the feeling for yourself.

To get started investing these days, you need either a regular investment of £25 per month with some platforms or £50/£100 one-off for the lowest entry platforms, usually the robo-advisers for the ISAs. Auto-saving apps also invest your spare change and they are very easy to use (micro-investing), and while what you invest may not be enough for retirement, it will help you to get started. However, it's important to bear in mind the cost of investing that I've explained above, especially when you invest small, because you don't want the costs to be higher than your potential gains.

AN IMPORTANT NOTE ON FEES

When looking at fees for buying and selling funds we need to talk about platform fees (the one holding your investment) and fund fees:

Buying/selling shares: Check whether you have to pay an account fee or a subscription. When you buy and sell shares, you pay a fee (reduced if you trade often or almost nil on some new commission-free dealing platforms – this can be anywhere between £0 and £15 per trade). When purchasing UK shares, expect to pay stamp duty above a certain amount. Some platforms also allow you to buy fractional shares (a portion of a share).

Funds: Look at the ongoing charges figure (OCF) – it's useful to compare the costs of funds, which are usually as follows: active funds: 0.75–1.25%; index funds: 0.25–0.85%; and investment trusts: 0.8–1.8%.[52] You will also have to pay fund trading costs and stamp duty, performance fees and fund platform fees (most platforms charge an ongoing admin fee – a percentage or a fixed fee).

When you use a robo-adviser, you don't pay the above fees directly but pay a percentage of the money you invest with them. The basic fee goes down when you increase the amount invested. It also depends on the level of service you choose.

How to choose funds

The important rule of investing is *never to put money into something you don't understand*. Spend a bit of time on it, researching and asking questions before taking the plunge. Professionals are always there if you're not sure. Many DIY platforms have a lot of online content (research, data, articles, videos about how to invest, what to invest in, market updates, etc.). This is a good place to start, at least with your own research. Check how they selected the funds. Some platforms even have filters to help you choose.

You can use the ready-made portfolios (the premium service offered by some investment platforms) and this is how I invested initially. If you are just getting started and lack a little bit of confidence, and also to save you the hassle of asset allocation, these can be a good option. Based on a risk questionnaire, the platforms suggest a portfolio of funds. Once your portfolio is built you have the flexibility to change it and add/remove some investments. Take your time to look into each suggested portfolio and really question everything (see below). All this is done online, you won't talk to anyone and have no pressure whatsoever to act fast; try to enjoy it and feel that you're in the driving seat.

Ready-made portfolios usually contain different types of funds, some equity funds, some bond funds and a bit of cash. Depending on your risk you will see more of one vs. the other. The ready-made portfolio could suggest five to fifteen funds you could buy, that have names such as FTSE100 MSCI, S&P500, EM Bonds; these are the **tickers of the funds** (a ticker is a symbol or abbreviation used to identify a fund or a stock). By clicking on these you can see a full description of what they are.

Once you decide it's time for you to invest, you can transfer money to your brokerage account (be it an ISA or SIPP, for example) then buy the funds suggested in the portfolio. Once you have bought them (it may take a few hours or days depending on what you buy) you receive confirmation and see the funds appear in your account. You can now just hold the funds until you decide to sell them in the long term.

With **robo-advisers**, this process is slightly different. You won't have to choose your investments – the robo-advisers invest your money for you in a lot of different funds, which you can then look up.

To help you find and understand investments in even more detail:

- Read financial news or the content on your investment platforms.
- When choosing funds, make sure you visit the fund providers' websites and read the factsheet/prospectus that includes a lot of information about the management of the fund, launch date, strategy and benchmark, fund size, fees, minimum investment, classes (growth versus income), the main fund holdings (diversification), geographic and sector allocation, etc.

- You should also check the past performance of funds and relative performance versus their benchmark for active funds.
- Check online platforms (such as Trustnet.com) to see fund prices, performance and key facts, and start comparing the funds.

Invest in what you believe in

We all have strong beliefs and passions, and we can use investing to reflect and support the things we care about most. An increasing number of us invest according to our values.

Sustainable investors with an environmental, social and governance agenda will look at the ESG practices of the companies that they invest in, and identify potential risks and opportunities associated with the non-financial impacts of the business. (Though beware: now corporations are coming under greater pressure to provide information relating to their wider responsibilities, some have engaged in the practice of 'greenwashing' i.e. using marketing techniques to (inaccurately) look socially responsible and mirror the values of ethical investors.) ESG investors are socially conscious but their main driver of their investment remains their financial returns.

Most robo-advisors offer sustainable portfolios using the principles of ESG investing and you can also pick funds that align with your values.

If you're interested in sustainable investing, I invite you to research socially responsible investing (SRI), impact investing, negative and positive screening, as well as becoming a shareholder activist.

Rebalance your portfolio

Maybe you had a specific asset allocation based on your risk profile per goal on Day One, but the markets are moving all the time, so your asset allocation is also moving. Prices of stocks tend to grow faster than bonds, so you could well end up with a higher proportion of stocks vs. bonds in your portfolio. You may also have had major life changes or decided on new investment goals. Perhaps it's time to rebalance your asset allocation? Check your portfolio at set intervals (e.g. every year) to make sure it's not going off-piste...this process is called 'rebalancing'. You can always ask for help with rebalancing from financial advisers or look at the robo-advisers or other model portfolio services that will be able to do it for you.

Ten Rules of Investing

1. **You cannot predict the future:** Your investments can go up, but they can also go down and you could lose money. Don't overreact! Only invest money you can afford to lose, based on your goals and risk appetite.
2. **Invest for the long run:** This means thinking in terms of ten years or more. Time is your friend.
3. **Make sure you invest as tax-efficiently as possible:** Understand your options: ISAs vs. pensions.
4. **Don't put all your eggs in one basket:** You don't want to lose it all. Diversify your investments to reduce risk.
5. **The more time you have, the more risk you could possibly take:** If you don't need the money for a very long time, you can usually take more risks. However, if you need the money sooner, you should definitely avoid this course of action.
6. **Invest in a low-cost way:** Always check the fees. Compound interest is fab, but fee cost compounding not so much.
7. **Review and rebalance your portfolio:** Your life, as well as the markets, changes all the time.
8. **Think about who can help you:** Don't hesitate to shout for help and never, ever invest in something you don't understand.
9. **Start small and invest regularly:** Slow and steady wins the race.
10. **Have fun but be boring in the way you invest:** You are not a trader but are looking for a boring, long-term successful investment strategy!

I hope this chapter has given you a basic understanding of how the markets work and how you could get started. *Knowledge is power, as is adopting an investor mindset.* Even if you decide only to invest small in a way that works for you, you can pat yourself on the back and know that you've come out of the shadows into the world of finance. It won't necessarily be an easy ride and you'll make some mistakes, but I hope you'll enjoy investing over time.

* *

CHAPTER 7
WANT TO
BUY A
HOUSE?

* *

What you will learn in this chapter:
How to develop a home-buying strategy
How mortgages work
The process of buying a house

* *

For generations, buying a home has been viewed as the ultimate measure of success, but home ownership among 25- to 34-year-olds has plummeted in the UK over the past few years. It's hardly surprising, given the insane rise in house prices, coupled with the fatalistic 'Why even bother?' attitude that many young people have now adopted in the face of these huge increases. But let's remain positive – after all, buying a home isn't just a financial decision, but an emotional one too.

Is It Worth It?

We know that buying a house is an expensive, long-term commitment. As with everything in life, both buying and renting have their pros and cons:

Some buying considerations	Some renting considerations
• When you pay off your home, it's all yours – you own an asset (and usually a large mortgage) but you are also financially responsible for repairs and maintenance	• Renting isn't 'throwing away money' as some would say – because you actually get a place to live
• If your house does increase in value, you can earn a return or break even. The opposite is also true – when house prices go down, you may lose money	• What you can afford as a tenant could be nicer and more spacious than what you can afford as a homeowner (especially true in urban areas)
• It could be cheaper to pay a mortgage than to rent but, if interest rates rise, you may end up paying more	• You run the risk of being made to move out by your landlord
• You could rent it out to generate some income (check the taxes)	• No need to worry about stamp duty, conveyancing fees, valuation fees, mortgage fees, repairs and maintenance... The list goes on
• Emotional security: owning a home is a tangible asset, so it has an emotional benefit, by making you feel secure and safe	• You don't have the same commitment as you would to your mortgage, allowing for more flexibility

Maybe the idea of committing to a mortgage is simply too stressful, or perhaps you'd rather own a modest home in the suburbs than rent in the middle of a city. If you're prepared to ride out a few fluctuations and stay in the game for the long haul, you should be fine. Ultimately, the decision to buy is up to the individual, but if you do want to, this chapter is for you.

Getting on the Ladder

Home buying can be a lengthy and overwhelming process with plenty of ups and downs, but it's all about preparation (and a little bit of luck). From setting yourself realistic expectations to understanding the importance of lenders' timings, here is the definitive checklist to buying a home in the UK.

In order to buy your home, you will need to save for a **deposit** and also borrow some money (usually with a **mortgage**) to cover the full cost of the house and buying fees. In basic terms, a mortgage is a loan you take out to buy a property. The loan is secured, which means that, until you pay it all off, the lender has an asset they will be able to rely upon, some sort of security in the value of your property (they do not own a share of the property). Worst-case scenario, if you can't repay the loan, the lender can take back ('repossess') the house to sell it and get their money back (mortgage lenders don't lend 100% to cover themselves for this possibility, but, in some cases, you could obtain 90–95% of the price of the property).

Where to start

- Build up your credit score (see page 13)!
- Register on an online property website to get property alerts. This will give you an idea of how fast-moving the market is in your preferred area. If only one house in your price range is coming onto the market every six months, you'll know you'd better pounce as soon as you're ready.
- Register on the electoral roll at your current address, as many mortgage companies use this to verify your identity.
- Start visiting places to get an idea of what you like and what you can buy within your value range. Talk to neighbours, and check out planning

permission posters on trees in the vicinity and on your council website to really get a sense of the area.

- Check the prices of houses that have recently been sold in the area. You can find this on the same sorts of websites listed above.
- Know what your trade-offs will be. For instance, you need to be open to discovering new neighbourhoods.
- Mind the lease length. If you're looking to buy in a city, chances are the property will be 'leasehold'. Leasehold is an ancient form of tenure unique to England and Wales, which essentially means you have a lease from the freeholder (aka the landlord) to use the home for a number of years. The leases are usually long term, but lately there's been an increase in short-term leases of 20 to 25 years. It may seem like a technicality, but the truth is that lease length is important, and it's worth seeking professional advice on what is best suited to your financial situation before taking a decision.
- Enjoy the process! Try out the local pubs, parks and cafés! Remember, this is a positive and exciting move – one of life's big adventures.

GET YOUR FINANCES IN ORDER

- **Start saving – you usually get the best rates with a greater deposit!**
- **Start paying off your debts. Credit cards and expensive loans should be top of your list when clearing your financial decks (see page 21).**

Find a good mortgage broker

In order to select your mortgage and find the best deal, you could apply directly to a bank and also use comparison websites.

A mortgage broker will give you their expert opinion on the best mortgage for you in terms of the interest rate and likelihood of your application being accepted. Mortgage brokers also have a view of market conditions and can definitely add value to the process. They will provide you with an understanding of how much the bank can lend you, what costs will be involved and who can actually lend you the money. Brokers could also have access to deals only offered to intermediaries (themselves) and not the public. They may smooth the mortgage process for you and buy you time: a good broker will also help manage the whole house-buying process.

It's smart to go for a brokerage firm with a long record of business in your area of the market. You should carefully vet these people both by checking on the FCA records and also by having a chat with them to see if they seem sensible and easy to work with and talk to.

Again, adding services can cost you money. Note that there are also online brokers now: these new disrupters on the market do the legwork of finding a mortgage for you, offer you online education and search all mortgages deals to find the most suitable one for you. The websites receive a fee when you complete your mortgage. Always make sure they are FCA authorized and regulated. After the selection process, there are still 'human' brokers to make sure your application is correct.

Saving for a Deposit

The first step is to start saving for a deposit. If this is one of your goals, you may already be working towards it. The more you can save to put towards your deposit, the less you borrow, and the less you borrow, the less you'll pay in interest. At the same time, what you should always keep in mind is that you don't have to put down the highest possible deposit because it's really important to retain a financial buffer.

When borrowing, it pays to show banks that you're good at controlling your spending and understand the importance of frugality, as they will want to see whether you can swallow unexpected costs if interest rates increase.

Options and schemes available

There are some government schemes available for first-time buyers that allow you to put together a smaller deposit than normally required – so you may be closer to home ownership than you think.

Help to Buy Equity Loan

The Help to Buy Equity Loan allows first-time buyers to purchase a newly built property with a 5–20% (5–40% in London) deposit (see the government website for the latest information and maximum property price).[53] You will need to instruct your solicitor or conveyancer – a person whose job is to manage the legal process of moving land or property from one owner to another – to apply for your government bonus, when you are close to buying your first home.

Help to Buy Shared Ownership

If you can't afford the mortgage on 100% of a home or love where you live and it's impossible to buy, the government has another scheme called Help to Buy Shared Ownership. Under this scheme, you purchase a share of a new build or existing property leasehold and pay rent on the remaining share. You can increase your share in the future to own a larger part of the property. This offers you the chance to buy a share of your home and pay rent on the remaining share. You can then pay the deposit with the money you save or take a mortgage for the share of the property you are buying (see the government website for the latest information).

Lifetime ISA

The Lifetime ISA is another way to save for a deposit for first-time buyers (see page 83).

Getting a Mortgage

How do mortgages work?

When you take on a mortgage, you borrow money (capital) to buy a property. In exchange, the lender charges you interest until you repay them in full. The *interest* you pay on your mortgage is the cost of borrowing the money; it defines how much you will be paying each month and over the course of the mortgage. Different mortgage providers also charge different interest rates.

You can choose to pay monthly interest *and* capital (a '*repayment mortgage*') or only to pay interest on your loan (an '*interest-only mortgage*'). With repayment mortgages, because you have been paying some interest *but also a portion of the loan* each month, your balance decreases with time, and at the end of the term you would actually own the property, which is not the case with an interest-only mortgage. Your monthly repayments with repayment mortgages will almost certainly be higher than with interest-only mortgages but at the end of the day (in 25 years!) you will actually own the place. Since you are repaying a portion of the capital every month, the interest you are paying will gradually decrease.

It's worth noting that since the credit crunch it has been harder (especially for first-time buyers) to get an interest-only mortgage.

EXERCISE

Use a calculator to determine how much you will have to pay every month on your mortgage.[54]

95% MORTGAGE SCHEME

This scheme is backed by the government and helps first-time buyers or current homeowners secure a mortgage with just a 5% deposit to buy a house of up to £600,000, hoping to facilitate access to property ownership for aspiring home owners. The scheme, launched in April 2021, is available on high streets across the UK. Unfortunately, affordability checks still apply which means you may not be able to borrow enough money. Make sure you check the rates on these higher loan-to-value mortgages to make sure you can afford it.

Choosing the right mortgage for you

Whichever mortgage you have in place, you can choose how your monthly payments are calculated:

- **Fixed rate mortgage:** With this type of mortgage you have the certainty of paying the same amount of money each month for a period of time, between two and ten years, regardless of how interest rates are moving in the meantime. At the end of the period you will be put on a *standard variable rate* (see below) which can be much higher, so then it may be time to look for a new mortgage.
- **Variable rate mortgage:** With this your mortgage payments go up or down in line with interest rates.
- **Tracker mortgages:** These move directly in line with the BoE's base rate. So it will cost you less when the base rate is low but your repayments can also go up if this increases.
- **Standard variable rate (SVR) mortgages:** SVR is the rate lenders charge you for the loan. They can decide to move the rate over time, usually following the BoE's base rate. That's not very helpful for budgeting. It can also be quite risky for you in case interest rates go up a lot and you are in a position where you can't afford your monthly repayments.

There are, however, three other types of variable rate mortgages:

1. **Discount mortgages** offer a discount on the lender's SVR – although not to the base rate. Banks fix their SVR for two to three years.
2. **Capped rate mortgages** move in line with the lender's SVR up to a cap, so the rate can't rise above a certain level.
3. **Offset mortgages** link your savings to your mortgage, so you only pay interest on the balance between mortgage and interest.

You can check the current base rate on the BoE website[55] and visit the MoneyHelper website for more details on all these mortgages.[56]

Choosing a variable over a fixed rate mortgage is a difficult and very personal choice. Fixed rates can be more expensive but they give you visibility of how much you will be paying over the years. Variable rates can cost less, but they can put you in a very difficult situation if interest rates go through the roof as you will become exposed to potentially very high monthly payments.

Make sure you shop around so you don't miss out on getting the mortgage that's best for you. This is a really crucial area where advice from a mortgage broker is invaluable. The same goes for the mortgage term.

BUYING WITH A PARTNER

Obviously you can get a bigger mortgage, and usually deposit, if you buy a home with your partner or someone else (from two to four people). Both your names will be on the mortgage agreement (this is called a *joint mortgage*) and you are both responsible for making repayments. If the other party can't make the repayment, you are also liable. This could also have an impact on your credit score, as you become associated financially with someone who has bad credit. You don't have to own the same percentage of the house, and that also affects how much you will need to pay off. In order to decide how much you will be able to borrow, lenders will look at your combined income.

How much can you afford to borrow?

Mortgages are based on how much you earn per month minus your expenses and any other debt repayments (including any loans or credit card debt). Lenders want to make sure that if they lend you money you will be able to repay them – and also pay the interest on your mortgage. Measures of *affordability* are becoming increasingly sophisticated these days but as a rule of thumb, income multiples are a better guide than anything else (a maximum loan of four to five times gross income), according to mortgage brokers.

There is an important metric called Loan-To-Value (LTV) that indicates the percentage of the value of the property that is covered by the mortgage. Subtract your deposit as a percentage of the property value from 100%. So, if you have a £40,000 deposit on a £200,000 home, that's a 20% deposit. This means you owe 80% – so the LTV is 80%.

The MoneyHelper website has a super-handy Mortgage Affordability Calculator that helps you understand how much you can afford to borrow by looking at your monthly income and your outgoings.[57] Mortgage lenders will look at these figures very closely to work out how much they'll offer you.

The mortgage application process

1. Prepare your paperwork and build a strong case

Depending on your personal situation (an employee or self-employed) you will need to build up a case to show exactly why you can afford to borrow. Lenders will want full details of your employment/self-employment, your existing loans or credit card debts, bank account details and, of course, full details of the property you want to buy.

You will need to have your payslips, P60 and bank statements handy. If you are working part time you may be earning less than someone full time and that can affect how much you can borrow, but you will be asked for the same documents as full-time employees.

For the self-employed securing a mortgage was traditionally a headache. Thankfully, the market is responding to the shift in work patterns and self-employed people nowadays have more mortgage options than ever before. You will need to get that paperwork prepped – you'll need to have two or three years' worth of accounts, as well as any associated tax calculations at the ready, as well as your Self Assessment tax return. Some lenders will consider your application if you are able to provide evidence of regular work or that you have work lined up for the future. Unfortunately, banks may be more hesitant to lend to people who are self-employed because it's a bigger risk than lending money to those who can show they are full-time employees.

Lenders will also check personal details: they will want to verify who you are and where you have lived for the past three years, so be prepared to show valid ID and official paperwork (council tax, utility bills, bank statements).

Lenders will review all the documentation you send and they will also have additional questions. You will usually have a meeting with the lender (or your mortgage broker if you have one) and they will ask about your understanding of the mortgage, and your capacity to borrow based on the documentation you provided. The goal of the meeting is to really understand if you can afford the money you are about to borrow. You should feel confident that you can and use the opportunity to ask any questions you have.

2. Submit your application

Mortgage agreements are really finicky legal documents, so try to fill in all the forms carefully and comprehensively. When asked to enter your name, include any middle names. You must check and recheck everything yourself to be sure there are no mistakes. If you are working with a mortgage broker, they won't generally send you a copy of the application; they have to check it for you.

3. The lender needs to value your property

This is a formality to enable them to compare the amount you've requested with the price of the property. Be aware that mortgage lenders are often less willing to lend against properties that might prove difficult to resell, should you default on your repayments; these can include flats above commercial premises or old buildings. This transaction can take up to a few weeks.

4. The lender has accepted...or not

If all is well, the lender will write to you and your solicitor (and your mortgage adviser, if you have one) confirming how much money they are prepared to give you and under what conditions. You will see on this letter all the details of the loan. Read that small print!

If your application is turned down, it could be that you don't have enough money saved as yet or that you're not on the electoral roll. Whatever the reason, don't be too disheartened. You can change all these contributing factors and try again in a little while.

5. The lender will issue a formal mortgage offer

Big moment! Copies will be issued to you, your solicitor and, if relevant, your mortgage broker.

6. Conveyancing

You can now start the legal process of 'conveyancing': transferring a property from one person to another. Your solicitor will also look at local authority searches. These are important because they include all the information relating to the area surrounding the property (for example, large developments nearby, road maintenance, planned new train tracks) collected and researched by the local authority. They can then send the Report on Title to the lender and arrange for the property to be placed under your name. This process can take four to six weeks.

7. The exchange
This is the last step of the process. All parties are happy with the sale and you can fix exchange and completion dates. At this point you need to be 100% sure of your wish to purchase otherwise you will lose your deposit and legal costs incurred. You have to pay a deposit before you exchange contracts. Things are serious – you've just made your biggest transfer of money.

8. Completion
You receive a completion statement from the solicitor that also lists all the money you still need to pay: outstanding deposit, stamp duty (within 30 days of completion, through your conveyancer or directly) and legal fees (see below). These will have to be paid on completion date which is also the day you finally receive the keys.

Well done, the place is yours!

The 'Hidden' Costs of Buying

- *Stamp duty:* Most people will have to pay this tax on the purchase. Make sure you check the current rules.
- *Legal fees:* The whole buying process costs money and you will need some help from a solicitor.
- *Council searches:* These are required for information such as planning applications and road information.
- *Surveys:* There are three types of survey: basic/valuation (usually the minimum as carried out by the lender), homebuyers' (for example, checking for things like damp and subsidence) and full structural. Full structural surveys are generally recommended for houses, with homebuyers' surveys perhaps more suitable for flats.
- *Fees on mortgage:* According to MoneySuperMarket you will sometimes need to pay a booking fee but not always, an arrangement fee (a fixed

sum or a percentage of the mortgage value) and a mortgage valuation fee (that is dependent on the price of the property).[58]

- *Broker's fees:* Depending on the agreement you have with your broker you may have to pay them a fixed fee or a percentage of the loan.
- *Land registry fee:* This fee is in order to register the property under your name.
- *Moving costs:* If this is your first home there is a chance you won't have a lot to move. However, there is a cost to rent a van to move your stuff or hire people to do it for you.
- *Life cover/insurance:* It is very important that you consider whether you will be able to keep the property should anything unfortunate happen to you. Life cover should be considered (sometimes it is required by the mortgage lender) as should buildings insurance (especially in the case of freehold properties).

REMORTGAGING?

A *remortgage* is a new mortgage on an existing property you own. You may want to remortgage for a few reasons: you have an old deal and you think you could get better terms and save money, or maybe you've been paying interest only and now want to start repaying the capital, or you want to borrow more to build a new extension, for example.

When remortgaging, always make sure you do the maths and understand all the fees. You will almost certainly be charged an exit fee or early repayment fee, but you also have to pay the fees associated with your new mortgage. Also make sure you can afford the new terms of the mortgage.

Should you overpay your mortgage?

The positives are that overpaying helps to remove some money from your bank account so you can't spend it, and you could significantly reduce your future payments. At the same time, though, if interest rates are low, ask yourself whether this is the best option or if you could do something better with your money (like contributing more into your pension or investing money).

Check the terms of your mortgage, but usually you can overpay up to 10% of your balance each year, without paying a penalty (check the small print on your contract for further conditions), helping reduce your monthly interest bill. It's not always possible and you may have to pay a penalty to do so.

If you want to use a calculator, go to the MoneySavingExpert website.[59]

What About Buy-to-let?

Buy-to-let is buying a property to rent it out to tenants. It is a long-term investment that you hope will pay you some income over time through rent and selling the property further down the line for (hopefully) a profit. Just as with buying a home, there is some risk involved: property prices can go up and down, tenants may not pay their rent or damage the property, and you must also consider the costs linked to managing and maintaining the property.

Remember that, when there is money earned, there are taxes to be paid! Always check the new tax rules on the government website.[60]

Mortgages designed for landlords (buy-to-let mortgages) are not the same as mortgages designed for homeowners (residential mortgages). These are the main differences according to MoneyHelper:[61]

- The fees as well as the interest rates with buy-to-let are much higher.
- Most buy-to-let mortgages are interest-only. This means you only pay interest each month, but at the end of the mortgage term, you repay the capital in full.

Please visit the government website to help decide if this is for you.[62] House buying is never going to be plain sailing – there's a good reason why people always say that buying and selling houses is one of life's mega stress-inducers! However, you're now well equipped to start the journey.

* *

LET'S CONTINUE OUR MONEY CONVERSATION

* *

I hope *You're Not Broke: You're Pre-Rich* will help you to overcome any fear of looking money in the eye and make you excited about starting to write your own money story.

Remember that rules change all of the time. Keep an eye out on the government website.[63]

The Vestpod community and I will always be here for you, so if you have a question and want to continue our money conversation, you can follow me on Instagram @vestpod. Visit vestpod.com for our weekly newsletter, articles and podcast *The Wallet*, and also register here for events and workshops.

I wish you well on your money journey. You really are in control of your financial future.

With love,

Emilie xx

Endnotes

Introduction

1 https://www.scottishwidows.co.uk/knowledge-centre/gender-pension-gap/

2 https://thepeoplespension.co.uk/wp-content/uploads/Measuring-the-ethnicity-pensions-gap.pdf

3 https://www.stepchange.org/women-and-debt.aspx

4 https://www.ftadviser.com/investments/2018/12/07/gender-investment-gap-estimated-at-15bn/

5 https://www.wbs.ac.uk/index.cfm/news/are-women-better-investors-than-men/

6 https://www.natsal.ac.uk/natsal-survey/natsal-3

7 https://www.independent.co.uk/news/science/talking-about-money-is-britains-last-taboo-10508902.html

8 Based on research by Dr Brad Klontz, a leading expert in financial psychology: https://www.psychologytoday.com/files/attachments/34772/money-beliefs-and-financial-behaviors-development-the-klontz-money-script-inventory-jft-2011.pdf

Chapter 1: Get Real with Your Money

9 https://www.nao.org.uk/wp-content/uploads/2018/09/Tackling-problem-debt-Report.pdf

10 https://www.gov.uk/repaying-your-student-loan

11 https://www.unbiased.co.uk/life/get-smart/cost-of-advice

12 https://www.fca.org.uk/firms/adviser-charging-rules

Chapter 2: Planning for the Future

13 http://images.mscomm.morningstar.com/Web/MorningstarInc/%7bb87a29d4-9264-4e6f-a5d7-5e65f8714f92%7d_US_ADV_MoreLess_Whitepaper_Final.pdf

14 The acronym first appeared in George T. Doran's article, 'There's a S.M.A.R.T. way to write management goals and objectives', *Management Review* (November 1981).

15 https://moneyandpensionsservice.org.uk/2020/11/09/21-million-money-scrts-kept-from-loved-ones-across-the-uk/

16 https://hbr.org/2005/03/off-ramps-and-on-ramps-keeping-talented-women-on-the-road-to-success

17 https://www.citizensadvice.org.uk/family/death-and-wills/who-can-inherit-if-there-is-no-will-the-rules-of-intestacy/

18 https://www.gov.uk/inheritance-tax

19 https://www.gov.uk/money-property-when-relationship-ends

Chapter 3: Own It: Get a Grip on Your Money

20 Warren, E. and Warren Tyagi, A., *All Your Worth: The Ultimate Lifetime Money Plan* (Free Press, 2006).

21 https://www.elle.com/fashion/shopping/a41845/shopping-dopamine/

22 Suggested by Kristin Wong: https://thegetmoneybook.com/save-money-and-time-with-the-1010-rule/

23 https://research.cornell.edu/news-features/intriguing-human-behavior

24 Anik, L., Aknin, L. B., Norton, M. I. and Dunn, E. W. 'Feeling good about giving: The benefits (and costs) of self-interested charitable behavior'. In *The Science of Giving: Experimental Approaches to the Study of Charity*, edited by Oppenheimer, D. M. and Olivola, C. Y. (Psychology Press, 2010). Retrieved from https://www.hbs.edu/faculty/Pages/item.aspx?num=36778 (accessed 14 Jan. 2019).

25 https://greatergood.berkeley.edu/images/uploads/Simpson-AltruismReciprocity.pdf

26 https://home.barclaycard/press-releases/2020/8/Lockdown-fuels-Subscription-Society/

27 https://www.moneyadviceservice.org.uk/blog/beware-the-vampire-economy-and-other-financial-frights

28 https://www.moneyhelper.org.uk/en/everyday-money/budgeting/how-to-save-money-on-household-bills

29 https://www.moneysavingexpert.com/reclaim/council-tax-bands-change/

Chapter 4: Asking for More Money

30 https://www.gov.uk/guidance/equality-act-2010-guidance

31 https://www.gov.uk/browse/business

32 https://hbr.org/2014/06/why-women-dont-negotiate-their-job-offers

33 https://www.tandfonline.com/doi/pdf/10.1080/23743603.2017.1309876

34 http://time.com/5312483/how-to-deal-with-impostor-syndrome/

35 https://www.gov.uk/tax-employee-share-schemes

36 https://hbr.org/2012/03/choosing-between-making-money

37 https://www.reed.co.uk/career-advice/part-time-pastimes-earn-brits-249-million-per-month/

Chapter 5: Navigating Your Bank Balance

38 https://www.gov.uk/browse/tax/income-tax

39 https://www.gov.uk/apply-tax-free-interest-on-savings

40 At the time of writing, but look out for potential changes to legislation in the future.

41 https://www.gov.uk/individual-savings-accounts

42 https://www.gov.uk/lifetime-isa

43 https://www.helptobuy.gov.uk/help-to-buy-isa/faq/

44 https://www.gov.uk/individual-savings-accounts; https://www.moneyhelper.org.uk

45 https://www.gov.uk/check-state-pension

46 https://www.gov.uk/plan-for-retirement; https://www.pensionsadvisoryservice.org.uk

47 https://www.moneyhelper.org.uk/en/pensions-and-retirement/pensions-basics/pension-calculator

48 https://www.gov.uk/find-pension-contact-details

Chapter 6: Investing for the Long Term

49 https://www.ons.gov.uk/economy/inflationandpriceindices

50 https://www.bankofengland.co.uk/monetary-policy/inflation/inflation-calculator

51 https://www.investopedia.com/articles/investing/062714/100-minus-your-age-outdated.asp

52 https://www.moneyhelper.org.uk/en/savings/investing

Chapter 7: Want to Buy a House?

53 https://www.ownyourhome.gov.uk

54 https://www.moneyhelper.org.uk/en/homes/buying-a-home/mortgage-calculator

55 https://www.bankofengland.co.uk/boeapps/database/Bank-Rate.asp

56 https://www.moneyhelper.org.uk/en/homes/buying-a-home/mortgage-interest-rate-options

57 https://www.moneyhelper.org.uk/en/homes/buying-a-home/mortgage-affordability-calculator

58 https://www.moneysupermarket.com/mortgages/first-time-buyers/cost-of-buying-your-first-home/

59 https://www.moneysavingexpert.com/mortgages/mortgages-vs-savings/

60 https://www.gov.uk/guidance/income-tax-when-you-rent-out-a-property-working-out-your-rental-income

61 https://www.moneyhelper.org.uk/en/homes/buying-a-home/buy-to-let-mortgages-explained

62 https://www.gov.uk/browse/housing-local-services/owning-renting-property

Let's Continue Our Money Conversation

63 https://www.gov.uk/money/personal-tax

Index

YOU'RE NOT BROKE: YOU'RE PRE-RICH

Thank You

To my brilliant editor Romilly and everyone at Octopus who believed in me in the early stages and gave me a chance to write this book. I am very fortunate to have had support from Leanne, Louise, Julia, Juliette and Mireille, and many others over the years and this book's various editions.

To the Vestpod team, especially Veronica and Melissa, who have helped me write the best words and ideas to get more women financially empowered. To all the experts I interviewed for this book and the podcast, and who are part of the Vestpod community – thank you for supporting me in this journey, you all make finance a better place!

To my tribe of advisers, The Family, mentors, friends, journalists, lawyers and start-up accelerators – the support you've provided me over the years has been invaluable!

To my dear Vestpoders, none of this would have been possible without you. Thank you for inspiring me; you continue to shape my vision every single day. I am so proud of what we're building together.

To my family and friends, for your unconditional support and love.

Octave, Archibald, Olivia and Charly – you are everything!

A big thank you, this book is all yours 😊.

About the Author

Emilie Bellet is the founder and CEO of Vestpod and host of 'The Wallet' podcast. Having previously worked in private equity and at Lehman Brothers, she launched Vestpod as a way of empowering women financially and in order to start breaking the taboo around money. Vestpod is a digital platform with a popular weekly newsletter as well as personal finance workshops and networking events.

Emilie is a columnist for the *iPaper* and her writing has appeared in the *Financial Times*. Vestpod has been featured on TV and in publications such as *BBC News*, *Financial Times*, *Forbes*, *Vogue*, *Harper's Bazaar*, *This Is Money*, *Glamour*, *Cosmopolitan*, *The Guardian*, *The Independent*, *Stylist*, *Sheerluxe*, *Refinery29*, *Monocle* and *Courier Magazine*.

Emilie is a public speaker and co-authored *The WealthTech Book*. She has been included in the Women in FinTech Powerlist 2019 ('Rising Stars') and is a finalist in the 2018 Women in Finance Awards ('Disruptor of the year').

Emilie lives in London with her husband and three kids.

Join me: vestpod.com

This **brazen** book was created by

Publishing Director: Romilly Morgan
Senior Editor: Leanne Bryan
Assistant Editors: Mireille Harper, Sarah Kyle
Art Director: Juliette Norsworthy
Editor for the Revised Edition: Julia Kellaway
Typesetter: www.theoakstudio.co.uk
Production Controller: Serena Savini
Sales: Marianne Laidlaw, Kevin Hawkins, Stuart Lemon
Publicity & Marketing: Megan Brown, Hazel O'Brien
Legal: Sasha Duszynska Lewis, Imogen Plouviez